Praise for Labeled

"In a world that loves to label, defining and categorizing others and then placing them neatly in boxes, Stacy Dickman's book *Labeled* sets women free. If you want to stop striving for significance in the eyes of others and rest in the assurance of God's love for you, let Stacy's encouraging words and biblical insight empower you to wear only one label—beloved daughter of the one true God."

—**Karen Ehman,** *New York Times* best-selling author of *Keep It Shut: What to Say, How to Say It, and When to Say Nothing at All,* Proverbs 31 Ministries speaker, and Bible teacher for First 5

"Using wisdom from Scripture, Stacy redefines the unhelpful labels women get stuck in. The concepts in this book align with current research in psychology on shame, vulnerability, and connection. Readers can maximize their experience with this book by reading it in community—the discussion questions promote openness and draw out the commonalities between women."

—**Stephanie Shell,** counselor, ThrivePointe Counseling

"Dickman writes in a way that includes each woman and takes her on a journey. The group discussion questions are pointed and thoughtful, encouraging readers to uncover who God truly says they are—princesses of the most high king. My hope is that every teenage girl (and grown woman) will read this book so that they will be able to name the labels society tries to apply to them and live in the freedom of who God says they are."

—**Sara Mosteller,** Director of Cinderella's Closet, southwest Ohio

"Sit down with your favorite cup of tea or coffee and enjoy this conversation with someone who wants you to see yourself as God does. Stacy delivers a much-needed word to our world. *Labeled* has the potential to be the catalyst you need to be transformed by the Holy Spirit. Biblically literate, clinically sound, and graciously delivered. Don't miss it!"

—**Rev. Jeremy Spence,** pastor and counselor, First Baptist Church, St. Paris, Ohio

"In *Labeled*, Stacy masterfully combats cultural norms with biblical truth. Her study and exposition of Scripture gives women a clear window into God's heart and a new lens by which to see themselves and live confidently within his design. It's refreshingly authentic, as Stacy doesn't simply share practical advice, but shares her own personal struggles. Sometimes, the only thing we need in order to experience a breakthrough is to know that someone else already has. If you're tired of living someone else's version of you, read this book and reclaim your identity as a daughter of the king!"

—**Shawn Spradling,** lead pastor, Center Pointe Christian Church

Labeled

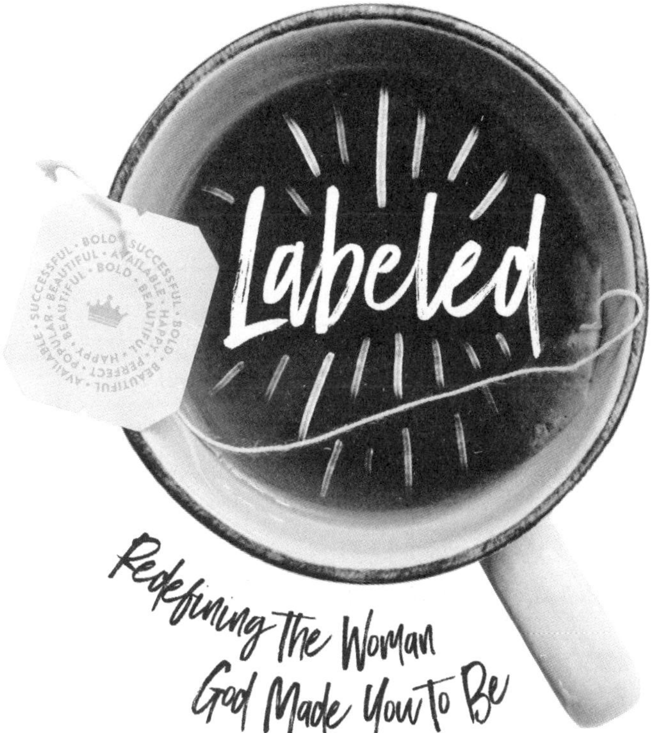

Labeled

Redefining the Woman God Made You to Be

STACY DICKMAN

LABELED

Redefining the Woman God Made You to Be

ISBN 978-1-68426-120-8
LCCN 2018020631

Printed in the United States of America

LIBRARY OF CONGRESS CATALOGING-IN-PUBLICATION DATA
Names: Dickman, Stacy, 1981- author.
Title: Labeled : redefining the woman God made you to be / by Stacy Dickman.
Description: Abilene : Leafwood Publishers, 2018.
Identifiers: LCCN 2018020631 | ISBN 9781684261208 (pbk.)
Subjects: LCSH: Women—Religious aspects—Christianity. | Identity (Psychology)—Religious aspects—Christianity.
Classification: LCC BT704 .D53 2018 | DDC 248.8/43—dc23
LC record available at https://lccn.loc.gov/2018020631

Cover design by Thinkpen Design, LLC
Interior text design by Sandy Armstrong, Strong Design

Leafwood Publishers is an imprint of Abilene Christian University Press
ACU Box 29138
Abilene, Texas 79699

1-877-816-4455
www.leafwoodpublishers.com

18 19 20 21 22 23 / 7 6 5 4 3 2 1

To Brian,

thank you for walking beside me

on this journey we call life.

Every adventure is grand with you.

Contents

Introduction

A Labeled Girl in a Labeled World

I stood in the middle of the room among the hundreds of business casual, stylish women, completely out of my comfort zone. I had traded my running shoes for a pair of nude-colored heels that lifted my five-foot-two frame one more inch from the ground. I had survived three days of mingling in this crowd of professional-looking women, and I looked forward to the yoga pants and hoodie waiting for me back home. The women's conference was kicking off its final day, and I put on my last round of business attire and headed out the door.

As I pulled up my seat, the woman at the adjacent table took me by surprise. She walked over to me and complimented my attire for the weekend, followed by the question, "Where do you shop?" I hesitated, looking down at the used gray suit coat and peach pants I had put on that morning. I had rolled up the sleeves of the jacket because they were a bit too short. The shirt underneath had a large stain on the side that you couldn't see so long as I left on the jacket. My hair was tied back, still wet from the morning shower I had barely squeezed in after oversleeping. I felt like a wreck, and I wondered if I could even answer the question.

The truth is, I am a thrifter. I'm a bargain hunter by nature, and I love to go to the local thrift stores to piece together a fresh look. Thrifting is fun for me, while helping me make the most of my family's budget. The outfits this new friend noticed in the three days prior had all been thrift store finds. My first instinct was to lie. I wanted to avoid a label. I wanted to be perceived as well-dressed, but not as someone who frequents thrift stores. I decided to tell her the truth about my clothing purchases and shopping preferences. I admitted that all my clothing had been secondhand finds or bargain store closeouts. To my surprise, she was thrilled to hear of my thrift store habit. My truth-telling encouraged her, sending her on a mission to find her own cute fashion without blowing her family's tight budget. I am glad I chose not to create a lie to make her think I had it all together.

In the moment, I wanted to avoid any situation that might associate me with the label of *thrifter*. I feared my friend might identify me as a woman in need, as having to shop at a thrift store to make ends meet. It's true—I often cannot afford department store prices and find myself needing the discounts of a secondhand store. Yet to admit my need as I try to blend into a crowd of women who seem to have it all together feels as if I am hanging a placard around my neck for all to see. It is a label that identifies me as less than I want to be.

Labels

Labels. Our world is molded around them. Nutrition labels. Clothing labels. Eco-friendly labels. We check the labels on our food to keep our calorie counts in check. Our clothing labels define our wealth, social status, size, and sometimes our age. Warning labels can prevent allergic reactions and protect our families. People even label their emails to distinguish between work and friends.

Labels help us sort the world around us. They create an organizational structure for our environment. By identifying labels, we can find what to eat, what to wear, and where to go. With the touch of a button on a label maker, we can print and stick labels to organize our stuff. But labels go beyond categorizing things, often categorizing people and behavior.

Labeling of people or behavior creates social precedence. It creates categories of moral and social acceptability. We often label behaviors as good or bad based on their social acceptance, so it becomes okay to act a certain way or participate in a certain activity because others around us are participating.

Columnist David Brooks suggests in his book *The Social Animal* that human behavior isn't defined by our ability to think and reason things out. Instead, he explains that human beings are social animals, not rational ones. We are essentially a product of our interactions, and as we develop socially, we begin to become ourselves. We try on a set of labels and learn from each other, and most of this is happening so smoothly that we never really stop and think about it. Our behaviors and definitions of ourselves are based on our social and relational perceptions. We pick them up naturally from our family, the people we meet, and the social world around us, defining who we are by what we think of these labels.

Not too long ago, I was hired to clean the classrooms at my kids' school. Once a week, I took out the trash and vacuumed in nine of the classrooms. It was a relatively easy job, except for the move from classroom to classroom. After each room, I hauled the trash, my cleaning bucket, and the enormous scrub brush that dangled the classroom keys through the hallway crowded with junior high kids—all while pushing the industrial-sized vacuum. I often felt like a bull in a china shop. I could certainly knock a few seventh graders over without even knowing it!

One day, I was walking through the halls with my extra-wide load when I heard a kid call out, "Make room for the janitor!" I moved over toward the lockers to get out of the way, but when I turned to look over my shoulder, I saw nothing. By the time I turned back around, I saw a clear path in front of me. "How nice," I thought. I took a step forward before I realized what had just occurred. I was the janitor.

My eyebrows raised and my face turned red, half in anger and half in embarrassment. I wanted to speak up in defense of myself, loudly declaring that I was not janitorial staff. So, I did what any level-headed person would do: I took a deep breath and ducked into the next classroom as quickly as possible, being sure to lock the door behind me. The negative thoughts I had associated with the label *janitor* conjured up strong emotion within me. At that moment I had no idea why, but later I saw it. My constructs of a janitor's work put the job in a lower social position than I wanted to hold. I thought I was better than a janitor.

The label of janitor seemed low-class. Less than worthy of a working mom trying to make tuition payments. I elevated myself above the title of a janitor and took up defenses when I was called one. But janitor is not a derogatory or degrading label. In fact, it's a busy, hardworking, and highly important position that is sometimes dirty for the advantage of others. Janitors and cleaning people work behind the scenes to better our schools and offices. The label of janitor should not have felt heavy, but complementary and suiting. I was a janitor, working for the good of the staff and students, and working to help support my family's involvement in the school.

Labels in the Real World

We are often dependent upon labels, many of which are necessary. The labels that distinguish my library books from the books in my own personal collection serve a valid purpose. I need these labels to help identify where each book belongs. These labels give me clarity. They keep me on track so I can be organized and avoid overdue fees.

When used properly, labels can make a substantial, positive difference in how we approach life. For example, labels can be extremely helpful when identifying a person's special needs: Allergic. Gifted. Autistic. ADHD. When labels answer questions or map out solutions, they are incredibly helpful.

But labels go beyond the helpful kind. People label people. Loser. Tiny. Tall. Religious. Goth. Rich. Arrogant. Overachiever. Tomboy. Talker. Fit. Workaholic. Weirdo. Nerd. Poor. Sick. We tag people with labels to help us decide where they belong. Labels are words that open a box so we can neatly tuck people into a category. We are quick to sort others by these labels and ready to compare ourselves to others within each box. We use labels to organize people into who we think they should be and how we compare to them.

Look around. Everywhere we go, we place people into the labels we construct. Each label has a place in the organization of our social world. The labels placed on each person assign a sum total of the person's value to us and our social world. The labels we deem as positive add value, and negative labels decrease our value. When we find that someone has a label we think is valuable, they become higher priority. We elevate them as worthier of our time and attention than others. We perceive this priority as importance. The more value I see in another's labels, the more importance they have, and therefore the more attention I will give. The opposite is true too. When I see another's labels to be less valuable, I choose to not spend my time on them. I turn my attention away in order to separate myself from the negative labels and decreased value they bring to my social circle.

We are assigned a social value based on how others label us, but we also have a self-given value reflecting the labels we place on ourselves. When our view of a label is something we see as good or popular, we quickly claim the label. We let it build us up and often even tell others about it. We begin to let it shape who we are, and even attempt to use it to fit into social groups and networks. We raise our standards because we perceive an added social value. At the same time, when we view a label as condescending or socially unaccepted, we allow it devalue us. A label can eliminate us from a group of friends or prevent us from reaching for a goal simply because we see a decrease in our social value because of it.

We strive to be valuable by earning or deflecting certain types of labels. Collecting labels that add to our value becomes a priority, and dispelling the labels that devalue us is important. We begin to create our self-worth—our identity—as it is defined by the labels we carry. If others call us smart, we feel the need to be smart all the time. A label of beautiful given by our suitor becomes a need to be beautiful every day for the rest of our life. We create an identity by the labels we allow and defend.

There are labels we work hard to earn. We put in hours and hours of work to achieve an executive status at the office in order to be called successful. We work tirelessly to create something special so that others will see us as creative. Or we smile all day, putting on our church face as if everything is fine, but cry all night into an empty pillow to carry the status of happy. These labels are often a reflection of what we prefer others to see, rather than an honest reflection of who we are. It's an identity we want to have. A label we want to fit.

Other labels we are desperate to avoid. We hide our thrift store pleasures and our outrageous coupon obsessions that save us money. The credit card replaces cash, we smile even when we don't think we can afford dinner, and the gas tank lingers on E until payday on Friday. We sweep labels like dust under the rug, hoping that not acknowledging them will somehow make them not true of us.

So often we create an artificial world to give ourselves control of the labels we do and do not want. Open your social media accounts and look at what you have posted. Scroll through the image you are portraying to the world. Do the words you tweet reflect the same words you speak to your coworkers and family? Do the images you post on Instagram echo your natural environment, or do you only snap a picture when things are perfect? Do you actually create the things you pin on your boards? The widespread use of social media allows us to influence our labels more than ever. I can choose to post inspiring quotes about living stress-free but sit at home each night fretting over the thirty-nine items on my to-do-by-Friday list. I can post a picture of homemade cookies I made this afternoon as I prop my feet on the overflowing pile of laundry. The world of technology and social media gives me some control over the labels I allow others to put on me.

The Permanent Ink: How a Label Impacts a Life

The labels from others help define our place among our peers. They create our social sphere and safe place. We tend to collect together in the boxes where we are most like others. It's like walking into a crowd and instantly feeling welcomed because you are all carrying a Kate Spade bag. This feeling of belonging naturally groups us socially. For example, one of my labels is "mom." The moment I walked into a Mothers of Preschoolers (MOPS) group, I fit. More often than not, I find myself in social circles with other moms. This safe zone makes me feel connected and valuable. It creates a space where I am welcomed. Being mom is not inherently good or bad, but its value is based on my context. When I am with other moms, it is an added value, but in some situations, it can decrease my value. No matter the situation, the label is always fitting. I will always have a seat at the table, and I belong here regardless of my skills or aptitudes at being a mom. I fit this label.

Because I am a mom, it is difficult at times to be wife. Mom in the context of a marriage relationship can be challenging. These two labels do not always neatly overlap. I undoubtedly fit both labels, creating competition within myself. At times, I find myself putting my mom cap on before I do my wifely duties. I put aside my book to sit and help my third grade son with his math homework, yet neglect to call out a greeting from across the room when my husband comes in the door from work. Or I allow guilt to cloud my mind when I choose to hire a babysitter and order pizza delivery for my children in order to have a date night with my husband at our favorite steakhouse. The labels mom and wife are both beneficial and accurate, but the competition between them sometimes leaves me feeling as if I am unsuccessful at both. They compete for attention, sometimes lowering my self-worth by the tension riding between them.

The competing nature of labels can affect our self-worth. The clash of academic standing and social group leadership can put us in the middle of a competitive set of labels. Home and work divide us, as do political affiliation, matters of faith, and socioeconomic status. The division between labels can pull us in many directions at one time, often leaving us to feel exhausted.

This competitive nature is true of the labels we attach to ourselves and the labels placed on us by others. We begin to use even our positive labels as something destructive, or something other than expected. Instead of a natural inclination toward the label "helpful," we begin to adjust our identity to fit the label as we want. Some of us will use the label "helpful" to seek out opportunities to be noticed. For others, every opportunity to live in a label becomes a hiding place. We change the definitions of who we are to match labels as we see value in them.

Our value begins to get lost when we are not using our labels the way God intended them. He created us in his image and for his purpose, and language offers words as a way to express the qualities he gave us. Every label we have is on purpose, but we can only find its value when we define it through God's perspective. When we look to cultural definitions and social values, we are redefining God's labels through a human lens—a lens that focuses on social values rather than kingdom values. We begin to assign a cultural identity to our worth, allowing what is socially relevant to define us. Doubts about who we are inch their way in when we feel irrelevant. When we don't fit in, it becomes a struggle to find happiness in any label, positive or negative. We feel less than enough. And when we feel less than enough, we seek to be more.

More of the labels that give me value. More of what I want others to see in me. More of what I choose to be my identity. My effort to be more in the world often interferes with my effort to be more of who I really am. My desire to be more "of the world" causes me to seek its ways rather than God's. I put my time and energy into the labels assigned by culture, neglecting who I am created to be. I buy the trendy outfits but forget to clothe myself with compassion. I update to the newest electronics but refuse to put them down long enough to pray in thanksgiving. And I laugh at the big screen hit but refuse to find the joy in my daily routines.

Some of us spend months, years, or even decades trying to be more. We begin eyeing the labels that make others happy. Women who have husbands. Women who have children. Women who have fancy cars and glamorous careers. We look for ways to be more like the women who have it all together and fit neatly in the box. We begin to do the things we think will allow us to be that kind of enough. And when we can't get there on our own, we start to bend our morals and bury our uniqueness to fit. We change our true self to be who we think we need to be.

For most women, this bending begins early in our teen years. We are told by the fashion industry how to dress. Books and movies tell us to act a certain way. We succumb to peer pressure to belong. And this becomes the norm. We begin to live a life seeking after what the world calls happy instead of what God calls "you." Into young adulthood, we follow the same route but begin to feel frustrated by our lack of ability to keep up. We give in to social media and instant access. We dream big dreams but try to reach them by following in someone else's footsteps. We bury ourselves in the false sense of happiness that comes with independence. It gets harder and harder to see who we were made to be as we become more and more who the world wants us to be.

Somewhere in life, we get knocked down by our fruitless efforts. We begin to notice that we are running hard, but not keeping up. We find ourselves surrounded by friends and all the stuff we can think of but feeling lonely. With one look in the mirror, we know in our heart the reflection staring back is not the person we were made to be.

Getting Back to Me

When we change who we are to gain or reject a label, we begin to lose who God created us to be. We are uniquely created and hand-designed by God the Creator. Everything about us is on purpose and for a purpose. God created our inmost being, knitting us together in our mother's womb (Ps. 139:13). Each detail of me is designed to be me. How I look, what I think, and the skills I have are purposefully given to me. The same is true of you. Every detail about you is made that way. You and I are made in God's image. It's our identity. By seeking after worldly labels, we deny our identity in him.

Sister, to be the woman God made you to be, you must first come face-to-face with the worldly labels you often strive to fit. You need to acknowledge the labels the world tells you that you should be, and search for what God expresses to you about each one. To be perfect, beautiful, successful, bold, popular, available, and happy are not poor qualities. Each label provides a piece of the definition of a woman in our world. When used properly, the labels give structure and organization to your identity. It is in the definitions assigned by the world that you see the changing and bending of the intended use into something different. Something less than beneficial. A definition that leaves you feeling less than enough.

In the summer of 2011, I was living the American dream as a midwestern, suburban housewife. I was raising my three precious children alongside my perfect husband in our cute, little three-bedroom house. My social media account boasted all the goodness going on: happy kids, beautiful house, and smiling adventures out and about. I worked tirelessly to fit all the molds of what the world told me I should be as a young mom. My life looked perfect. It looked beautiful. It fit the definition of an ideal woman in every way. Except for God's way. I had little confidence and no feeling of completeness. I desperately lacked joy. In essence, I was a worldly girl with no true identity.

Life began to fall apart that Thanksgiving. Issues beyond my family's control caused us to lose our home, and I became ill to the point that I was not allowed to stay home alone with my kids. A stay-at-home mom with no home and no kids is useless. The perfect world I lived in shattered, leaving me so broken I didn't know up from down. The image I had created for the world to see me as the ideal woman disappeared in a moment's time.

I faced an unknown me. I needed to identify myself without any of the worldly things I once had. I began to ask myself a lot of questions. Who am I when my world falls apart at my feet? Am I valuable if I don't appear to have anything of value? Can I be a daughter of the king if I have no relevance to the world? It was during these days of struggle I began to ask God what it means to be a woman. I wanted to know how he defines me and what he expects of me. I dug deep into the Word to discover whether or not the things the world tells me have any merit in who God says I am.

What I found changed me, as God's Word always does. I began to see expectations of the world fall to the qualities I already have within me. I found women in the Bible who did not have it all together but who used what God had made for his glory. I wanted to be a God girl. I wanted my identity to be in Christ and not in this world.

He made us unique. He made us on purpose and for a purpose. Whatever specific purpose that is, it is definitely not to be who others tell us we should be. He created man and woman to be his masterpieces, the ones he would love for eternity no matter what the circumstance.

I want to show you the different definitions that God has for each of these labels and how he wants us to use them for his purposes. When we begin to separate the world's definition from the intended purpose given by God, we begin to find an identity as a woman of God.

We find the ability to let go of the need for a label so that we can grasp the qualities already planted in us. Labels become a place we fit rather than a place we reach for.

Many women wrestle with these words as if it were a competition. We fight the battle of being enough. Smart enough. Beautiful enough. Good enough. It's as if there is a threshold of how much of each label we are supposed to have. We want to gather up as much of it as we can, and we fight tooth and nail to keep hold of it. Our labels become a collection, as if we can put them on display to prove to the world our value.

When we stop to look at the Biblical definition and intended use of each of these seven words—perfect, beautiful, successful, bold, popular, available, and happy—we can begin to restructure our view. We can reconstruct our self-worth and identity based on how we properly fit into each label. Our journey through each word will explore its worldly use and the pressures it creates. We will look at the misunderstandings that devalue us, why we continue to cling so tightly to them, and how to break free from the need to continue collecting more and more. We will look at God's intentions of how each word can and should be used to honor him, find a Biblical example of how to live within the label, and peek in at Scripture to better understand each word as defined by God. We will investigate the value each label should add and discuss how to live each one as we look to be women of God.

The labels God has for each of us serve a unique purpose. When we tap into these resources God created in the way he intended, we become faithful women of God. The labels we so often use to shape our presence in the world can be refocused as part of our core identity. They are gifts from God, not to be hidden away, but to be used in his way.

Let God open the boxes you have constructed so you can be labeled his wholeheartedly.

Discussion Questions

1. Often, labels create a space where we feel valued. What labels have created a safe zone for you? Where do you feel connected and valuable?
2. Sometimes two labels overlap to tug us in different directions. What two labels do you connect with that sometimes compete? How do you find balance?
3. Each part of you is designed exactly the way God intended you to be. He has designed your look, your thoughts, and your skills. What has God purposefully given you to use for his good? Are you currently using those resources the way he intended? Do you find yourself using your gifts in ways that do not glorify him?
4. Do you identify with the seven words we will explore? On which do you stumble the most? What other words leave you feeling less than enough?
5. Write a prayer asking God to open your boxes as you take this journey. Record your prayer and then reflect back on it at the end of this book.

Thoughts and Reflections

1

Perfect (adj): being entirely without fault or defect; satisfying all requirements; corresponding to an ideal standard or abstract concept.

Every year when the holiday season arrives, I find myself waiting for perfection to knock on my door. I dream of the beautiful fall colors and perfectly dressed scarecrows adorning my porch. I envision richly colored table centerpieces and perfectly placed pumpkin decorations. I imagine beautiful snow-covered evergreens and a Christmas village of small-town perfection. I can almost see the matching wrapping paper and delicately placed bows on the perfectly arranged stack of presents under the tree. The perfect holiday scene is right in front of me on the cover of my imaginary magazine, and my dream of making it come true is waiting for the knock.

My waiting for holiday perfection comes every year. I can visualize all the cozy details, from how it looks to how people will react. I think of it like the Crate & Barrel commercial of 2017, where Reese Witherspoon, an actress and mom, is interacting with her guests as they comment on all the details of her perfect Christmas party. But, unlike Ms. Witherspoon, I want to skip the part of perfect that comes in the practicing. I want perfect to arrive without the work involved.

One thing about the holidays I do love is the giving of well-thought gifts. I love the idea of special, handmade Christmas gifts selected just for the recipient, and I typically attempt to do something special for my family and friends. I sometimes choose grand gestures or gifts that are a bit big for me. I attempt to do something I have never done before in hopes of satisfying a family member or friend. I pull out all the stops to be perfect on the first try to create something special. And I always seem to fall short.

One November, my mom asked me to freshen up a Christmas wreath to hang on her front door. I love to craft and create, so I eagerly agreed. I worked with the materials she had picked and crafted a brand-new look for the wreath. When I finished constructing the project, I hung it on an interior door in my kitchen to keep it safe until I could deliver it. For days I walked past this newly dressed wreath and critiqued the final product. I found flaws and failures at every glance. A piece out of place, a bow tied off-center, or a branch protruding out too far. The more I looked at the wreath, the more flaws I found.

I continually worried this wreath redo was not good enough. It did not live up to my expectations, and in my mind, it surely was not good enough for the front door of my mom's house. I convinced myself I was a terrible crafter and that mom would not like my work. I worked up so much concern about the wreath's lack of perfection, I broke down and cried. I no longer wanted to give it to my mom. She deserved better. Not just a better wreath, but a better daughter who could craft better things.

Mom's Christmas wreath redo became my moment of realization: my desire to be perfect is creating a problem.

A World of Perfect

Perfection is a particular burden for me: heavy, awkward, and uncomfortable. I often find myself bearing the weight of seeking perfection. I want my house to be perfectly hospitable for visitors, as if there is never a pair of shoes in the middle of the living room. I want to cook the perfect meal for my significant other. I want my children to have perfect manners and my marriage to be an easy walk in the park with no disappointments. I want to look like the perfect woman who has it all figured out.

My need to live the perfect life spills into every task and every turn of my world. Relationships. Living and working spaces. Jobs. Finished products I can hold, and even the reputation I display. The desire for perfection presses into each one. How well I manage to reach perfection in each area adds up to creating my perfect life. Likewise, any inability to achieve perfection in each area pulls me further away from that life. I become a failure. I swing back and forth on the continuum of perfection and failure. The constant tug between them is exhausting.

Perhaps you can relate to my perfectionism and its all-or-nothing mind frame. Good is not the same as great, and great is always the goal. Very rarely, and only with significant effort, can perfectionists settle on the good when great is the desire. If we didn't meet or exceed the expectations, we failed. We can't cut it. We aren't good enough. We let this pattern of all-or-nothing thinking flow into nearly every area of life. I am not good enough at school because I failed the math quiz. I am not good enough at work because I did not make that one sale. I am not good enough at home because I forgot to put the laundry in the dryer. Sometimes the one task that did not go perfectly becomes our cue that nothing we do is good enough.

According to *Psychology Today*, the lens of perfection causes us to see life as an endless report card.[1] We perceive the world to grade us for our accomplishments or for the way we dress. Every move, every project, and every look becomes a reflection of who we are and what we are worth. Every person we encounter is giving us a grade. Forming their opinion. Judging. The constant fear of failing leads to a continuous fight or flight type of response. We go all-in, or we run away. Perfection-seeking individuals are often more motivated by the fear of failure, in their eyes or another's, than by the desire to achieve a goal.

Perfection-seeking that reaches into all areas of your life is debilitating. It keeps you from working toward an end result. Just as unhealthy is the perfectionism that sneaks in one project or place at a time. Perhaps you do not struggle with the need to feel perfect in your physical appearance, but you strive desperately to have a home perfect for entertaining and hosting. Maybe you have no desire to make a perfect meal, but you refuse to accept a small stain on your son's favorite shirt because your image must be flawless. The sink full of dishes may not bother you at all, but your being two minutes late to yesterday's meeting plagues your mind. Perfection can be widespread or hyper-focused. It can cover many areas or be concentrated to just one. Both create in us the internal battle between good and perfect.

When we strive for such a high bar, we tend to fall short of what our minds have conjured up. We expect we should be able to perfectly decorate our home like Joanna Gaines and whip up the perfect pecan pie like Paula Deen. We dream of making cakes like Duff Goldman or walking with perfect elegance like Duchess Kate. Our standard is TV-ready. When our world looks less than cover-ready, we focus on the things that are wrong. We highlight our mistakes and draw attention to the shortcomings. We often stop before we finish and continually critique the work we put in. Instead of pressing on to complete our projects, we allow the imperfections to stop us in our tracks. We set up camp thinking of all the missed words, less than par work, or hurt feelings we unintentionally caused. The pile of half-done work or "should have" thoughts begins to mount, leaving us feeling even less "good enough." Our inability to complete even one thing reproduces the feelings of inadequacy that keep us from moving forward.

This never-ending cycle of attempting to be perfect or produce something perfect leads us to feel incredibly flawed. We begin to believe we are worthless and unfixable.

We think of ourselves as broken and irreparable, and we are left feeling defeated. We simply fail to be the perfect wife, mom, daughter, sister, or friend. Admitting we don't have it all together feels like announcing defeat in the role of womanhood. And this feeling of defeat causes shame, which drives us to a place of hiding. It leads us down the path to a game of pretend. Instead of admitting defeat, we begin to pretend to be what we want to be. We put out our best images and stories for the public audience, pretending to be the perfect woman we only wish we could be.

But when we look perfect, we appear fake. We lose our true identity to an image, continuously building it to be better and better. Soon we look like a replica of the perfect woman. This false representation of our world creates a hierarchy where we unintentionally imagine ourselves as better than others because we appear to have it all together. Friends begin to pull away because they don't feel like they are good enough to be with us, while inside we feel like our imperfections are driving them away. This disconnect based on inaccurate representations of our lives can create distance in some of our relationships.

Think about Christmastime. How many photos do you snap before everyone has their eyes open and is looking in the right direction? Do you post any of the not-so-perfect, closed-eyed, non-smiling pictures on Instagram? Do you share the stories of burnt dinner rolls and forgotten gifts, or do you only post the fantastic pie you purchased at the local eatery? Where in your life are you hiding your true identity? Are you putting a perfect image out there, when your real life feels more like standing in a hurricane with a tiny umbrella?

The image of perfection is like the mirage of an oasis. It's a bending of the light that creates an illusion—a body of water in the middle of a hot, dry desert that gives you false hope. It looks just like the thing you need, but it's only a reflection caused by differences between the surface and air. Perfection looks like the thing we need. We make it our goal, but it's not really there. Perfection is only a mirage you find in the space between reality and a dream.

Strive is an action verb we use in the English language to describe a considerable effort. We strive for big goals. We dedicate time and energy to reaching them. You can say we often strive for perfection. We put time, effort, and energy toward reaching flawlessness. In the book of Ecclesiastes, Solomon writes, "What do people get for all the toil and anxious striving with which they labor under the sun?" (Eccles. 2:22). We continue to pour in the effort, but what are we achieving? What reward do we get for hosting a perfect party? What do we earn for making the perfect cake? What do we achieve when we post the perfect family photo? The result of our efforts is often minimal: We get a few pats on the back or a few likes on social media. We get a moment of recognition. Our result is a momentary "well done" that leaves in a flash, and such fleeting accolades will not sustain the inner depths of our identity.

When we cling to perfection, we are seeking approval. Recognition and admiration become the evidence of a job well done. But chasing the approval of other people is anxious striving. Solomon answers his question in Ecclesiastes 2 by reminding us that those who please God are given wisdom, knowledge, and happiness, but those who store up wealth on earth turn it over to God's people in the end. Compliments and likes may feel good. They may build up your bank of confidence and create a sense of wealth. Maybe a storehouse built on the acceptance of others makes you feel rich. Storing the approval of others may be wealth for the moment, but it is the gift of God's approval that leads to more.

In 2006, social media raised the bar on our image of perfection to a new level with the launch of Pinterest. With more than 175 million active subscribers, Pinterest has become the go-to place for inspiration and project ideas. People who have created beautiful works of art or amazing products can now display their efforts worldwide on the virtual bulletin boards of cyberspace. Others pin, comment, and share, providing plenty of acceptance. Pin after pin magnifies the desire for perfection. Spend more than five minutes browsing the billions of pins of magazine-worthy homes, photos, families, outfits, and art projects, and you will find a new, intense expectation of perfection.

Perfect to the world is flawless. Pinterest is a display of flawless projects and images. Brides want perfect weddings with gorgeous sunsets and beautiful centerpieces. Working women wish for jobs with no tedious tasks and coworkers who become best friends. We want faces with even skin tone and no wrinkles. We lust for our world to be smooth sailing. No cracks, no tears. No problems. Flawless.

Perfect by this definition is unachievable. For behind every perfect image pinned to a board are several practice attempts. And every perfect relationship you see pays its consequences behind closed doors. From failed art to failed relationships, striving to make our lives fit into the label *perfect* is like running on a hamster wheel that gets us nowhere. In fact, some psychologists believe that setting a goal of perfection is detrimental to making progress. We must set goals to be realistic and achievable, not flawless and without error.

How can we be satisfied with good enough in a world of perfect? To set ourselves free from the human desire of perfection is hard. Approval of others is the groundwork for friendships and social status. It is easier to put on our perfect images than to be real and authentic. Pretend is often easier than not good enough.

Good Enough: From Flawless to Complete

To be enough, we need to reshape the idea of perfect from flawless to complete. We need to stop striving for perfection and begin seeking wholeness. We refocus our idea of perfect from what we can do to what God can do through us.

The Bible provides three distinct uses of the word *perfect*. First, in the Mosaic law, perfect is used to describe the nature of the animals to be used for sacrifice. Sometimes translated as unblemished, the idea of a perfect animal is related to its value. Animals with proper form and health provided monetary value or worth. An animal for sacrifice should not be the runt of the pack or an animal that means little to the owner. To give an animal that has no value is to give nothing. A sacrifice must cost something. Typically, it would be the best animal the owner possessed. He was required to give his best—or perfect—animals as a sign of his trust in God to continually provide.

Second, perfect is used to describe people who are not in want. The Hebrew word *tam* and its related word *tamiym* are translated as perfect, blameless, upright, content, whole, sincere, or undefiled. Noah is described as blameless because he walked with God (Gen. 6:9). He held a sincere faith. Jacob is called content because he lived the life God provided and did not desire to change it (Gen. 25:27). He felt complete or perfect in living the life he had. The woman in Song of Solomon is referred to as perfect because she is undefiled or unchanged, not unblemished (Song of Sol. 6:9). This use of perfect refers to a sense of wholeness or devotion rather than the idea of flawlessness.

The third use of the word perfect in the Bible refers to being complete or finished. The Greek word *teleios* is translated twenty times as perfect or mature. It implies not a flawless characteristic, but rather something that has grown or been made whole. It is full and complete, lacking nothing from its intended totality. In one example, the Gospel of Matthew records for us an interaction between Jesus and a rich young man. The young man approached Jesus to ask what good thing might benefit him in the gaining of eternal life. Jesus said a man must obey what God has commanded. This young man then claimed to be an obedient follower, yet he continued to ask Jesus to identify where he lacked. Jesus replied, "If you want to be perfect, go, sell your possessions and give to the poor, and you will have treasures in heaven. Then come, follow me" (Matt. 19:21).

This young man claims to have lived a faithful life following the commandments and laws, but he appears to feel as if he is just not good enough. He is looking for an edge—that one thing he can do that will guarantee he is enough for God. He must have been shocked at Jesus's answer. To be perfect—to be completely faithful and wholly God's servant, to be mature in your faith—you must give up the world you have collected. This will be the way to treasures in heaven and eternal life. And everything you do after you give up your own world should be to follow what he is doing.

Would your jaw drop, too? Would you concede like the rich young man, turning back to your storehouses of earthly goods? Are you clinging to your world of perfect with white knuckles, missing the completeness and wholeness he has for you? Do you find yourself looking for the one good and perfect thing that will guarantee you are good enough for him? Jesus did not lay out a twelve-step plan of perfection with exact details. He didn't promise eternal life in just ten minutes a day. And he certainly didn't say anything about a comfortable life. If you want to be whole, you must give up your perfect world. The things we collect and consume in our attempt to be enough in this world are often the same things that block our growth and maturity in Christ. If we are not willing to give up our perfect possessions, we cannot find the satisfaction of being whole in Christ.

Can we have eternal life by following God's commands? Yes! But in merely following the law, we miss out on the complete blessings that come with a mature faith. We miss the peace that steadies us in the waves of the storm. We miss the joy given to us in the losses we may suffer. And we miss the fullness of life God has promised to those who follow him. The author of Hebrews tells us that it is by his sacrifice he makes us perfect forever (Heb. 10:14). It is because Jesus bore the cross that those of us who walk faithfully with God can be whole forever. By giving up perfection on earth and following Jesus, we can be whole and complete in our everyday life.

I Am Complete

A perfect life is a complete life. Living complete is part of our identity in Christ. It is who we are meant to be. Because when we are complete, we are made flawless through him. We cannot achieve it on our own. We must give up our own ideas of perfect for his gift of flawless. To be complete in him cannot be earned but given. It is the core of our God-centered life rather than the focus of our self-centered world.

Colossians 3:14 says this: "And over all these virtues put on love, which binds them all together in perfect unity." Love is the finishing thread for believers. Compassion, kindness, humility, gentleness, patience, and forgiveness are made complete with love. Every imperfection can be held together with the thread of love. If we can trade our image of perfect for an attitude of love, we can live a complete life following after Jesus. A perfect life in him.

When we love with our whole self, we give our best efforts. And like the Christmas commercial or my mom's wreath, we practice. We keep working until we make it a gift of love. My mom's wreath was a gift of love. Everywhere I found an error, she saw love. It hung front and center over her fireplace that season because she wanted it where she could enjoy it. My "not enough" became her family room focal point because it was made complete with love and kindness.

Living a Perfect Life

How do we make perfect our identity and not just create an image? Continuous effort. We must practice growth and maturity, aiming to give up on flawlessness and be content in wholeness. Here is how you can practice living a life of completeness:

- **Acknowledge the great and accept the good.** When you do something great, it's okay to acknowledge it. But you need to nod your head to the good, too. Let good be good.
- **Let go of stuff.** Don't hang on to your material things. Give up your possessions to make room for the blessings God has in store, and let him fill up what you lack.
- **Follow Jesus.** Don't chase after flawlessness; chase after the one who is flawless. If you follow the path to a perfect world, you will miss the path to God.

- **Give love, not greatness.** When you do something for others, do it with an attitude of love. It may not be great, but when done with love, wonderful things can happen.

Discussion Questions

1. Tell of a time you felt the need to make something perfect. What was the result?
2. Discuss your social media profile in comparison to your daily life. Are you putting on a front?
3. Talk about a project you almost didn't deliver because you worried about its flaws. How was it received?
4. In what area of life do you struggle to be good enough?
5. *Perfect* is used in Scripture in three ways: unblemished, content, and complete. Discuss the differences and how they apply to your life.
6. Jesus told the rich man to sell everything and follow him. What is something you have collected in this world that Jesus is asking you to give up to be complete in him?

NOTE

[1]"Perfectionism," *Psychology Today* website, accessed March 24, 2018, http://www.psychologytoday.com/us/basics/perfectionism.

Thoughts and Reflections

2

Beautiful

Beautiful (adj): having qualities of beauty; generally pleasing.

"You are beautiful! Oh my, I couldn't take my eyes off you as you walked across the room."

I'll never forget the spark inside me when I heard these words. They came from the lips of a more experienced woman as I entered a weekend conference a few years ago. My knees were quivering. My smile was timid at best. I attended the conference alone, with only anxiety and loneliness as companions. Not knowing another person in the room, I walked straight to the registration booth, entirely focused on not tripping over my never-worn-before heels. When I turned from the desk, I reminded myself to lift my chin and smile, and I took a deep breath. I begged my stomach to stop doing flips, searching deep inside for every ounce of confidence I could muster.

Her voice cut through the static noise in my head at that moment. My heart raced as I tried casually to look over my shoulder and see who she was addressing. She gently laid her comforting, warm hand on my trembling arm and introduced herself. Her southern accent and ladylike charm eased my anxiety in ways I can't explain. She was a God-given encourager with the exact words I needed to settle my spirit and spark the fire inside me.

The confidence her words ignited in me lasted well beyond the three days of the conference. To be called beautiful by a stranger—a female stranger—blew my mind. For weeks, I wondered why she thought I deserved that label. I was an ordinary woman with nothing unusual about me. I looked around the room and found many, many other ordinary women. I saw each of them as beautiful and unique. Many of them deserved the label beautiful, but I felt like a nothing in my own comparisons.

My eyes could see the tremendous beauty of the crowd of godly women gathered around me, yet my mind refused to admit myself into their company. I was present with them, but I did not belong. I was an outsider looking into the crowd. My new friend's words told me differently. She welcomed me as if I belonged. She purposefully made me feel beautiful in the crowd.

Models and Media: How Our Eyes Define Beauty

What defines beauty, and why did I apply the definition to women around me but not to myself? Beauty is a look. It's a surface-level appearance. Everywhere we look, we find a visual definition of beautiful. Media and retail quickly supply us with the ever-changing images of fashion. Beautiful through the years has been idolized by the look and design of clothing, makeup, and hair.

In the 1940s, beautiful equaled high-waisted skirts, skirts sitting at the knee, and pantsuits with a hat and gloves. Clothing shaped a woman as an hourglass figure, with wide shoulders and a skinny waist. Hair was pinned in place, and makeup accentuated the natural elements of the face.

The 1950s brought excess and dressing for wealth, as women began to spend more money after the war. This decade produced straight mid-calf skirts and soft shoulders that highlighted a woman's curves. The addition of mascara to a woman's makeup bag added accent to the eye, while the popularity of red lipstick gave attention to the fullness of a lady's lips.

The 1960s shortened skirts and transformed to an A-line shape for a disappearing waist. Moving from Jackie Kennedy's tailored look to the youthful fashions of Brigitte Bardot, this decade brought a playful style to the everyday dress code. Hairstyles lifted higher, and patterns became bolder.

Seventies fashion ranged from fringe and fur to bright tie-dyes. Skirt lengths varied, pant legs widened, and style was loud. Hair was let loose, and skin became acceptable.

In the 1980s, the trend shifted to pants, belts that narrowed the waistline, and the disappearance of necklines with the popularity of tube tops. Crimped and permed hair raged.

Babydoll dresses, flannels, silk shirts, and denim brought in the 1990s. Mall bangs were teased high and sprayed with enough hairspray to put a hole in the ozone layer. From the dark grunge look to the iconic look of *Beverly Hills, 90210*, fashion became a personal expression.

Fashions in the early 2000s lowered our pants to the hips and dropped our necklines to plunging. Spaghetti straps and super-short shorts ruled the young, while layers and maxi dresses surged in the slightly older generations. Pixie cuts and beach waves in our hair complimented the style.

Exposed shoulders, skinny jeans, bell sleeves. Colorful hair, glossy lips, and lined eyes. The trends of fashion come and go, leaving us caught up in the "now" mentality to find our definition of beautiful. Models trot the runway with up-and-coming fashions and advertise the latest trends on the covers of magazines. Social media gives us insight into the popular looks and newest takes on style. Even bloggers and vloggers weigh in on their takes of the newest looks. Fashion changes quickly, and the social definition of beauty often follows closely behind.

Walk into any women's clothing store, and you will find displays full of what the fashion industry approves as beautiful. The fit, the color, the pattern. Every detail about the clothing we buy is made and sold to fit an image. Retail is centered around the money, so what sells is what you see on the rack. What is on the rack is what goes on bodies. The look on the bodies and how it is collected becomes what is beautiful. It becomes a cycle of images. A circle of beauty. The circle influences our view, and our views influence the circle. We feed the circle with our buying power.

From the rising of the hemline to the falling of the neckline, fashion is persuading us that less is more: less coverage of our body is more sexually appealing. Exposing skin is in style. More thigh, more shoulder, a bare midsection, and even sheer tops have captured the trends. The revealing of skin often shows the physical beauty of the body. The dressing or undressing of our body creates interest and turns heads. It's the sex appeal factor of beauty. The desire to be attractive is a function of human nature, an inherent desire to impress and to get attention.

If something is in style or a popular trend, many women will choose to wear it even if it makes them uncomfortable. Let's face it: most of us do not find high heels to be comfortable. Yet their ability to visually lengthen our legs outweighs the consequences of aching arches that we will undoubtedly have at the end of the day. Attracting attention with our physical bodies is often defined as beautiful. Look at any red-carpet event, and you will see Hollywood elite using their bodies to get attention. From the cut and color of the dress to the message each ensemble is giving, red carpets are a place for women of fame to gain attention with their bodies. The same is true in our everyday world, from the cut and trim of formal dresses to increasing tightness in our everyday clothing. Our clothes and body language are often intentionally chosen to turn heads. Our bodies are a physical expression of beauty we use in many ways.

Women want to be liked and thought attractive. We want to be a part of something. Our hair, our clothes, and our hangouts are purposefully chosen as a way to gain acceptance. We use our clothing and other accessory choices as a means to be noticed. For example, if I have a day at home, I pull out my sweats and the fuzziest hoodie I can find. Or I am hanging out in my T-shirt and shorts. I dress for comfort with minimal thought about how I look to others. But if I have somewhere to go, I dress in a different way. I toss on my jeans and switch the hoodie for a sweater just to run to the big-box store up the street. I fuss in my closet to find the right outfit for a date night. I sort through shoes and accessories before choosing the right ones to wear to the coffee shop with my friends. I am continually thinking about the image I am portraying to the people around me.

This progression of thought as we get dressed and ready for the day is a natural rhythm. It allows us to think through the expectations of what is to come. We want to feel good about our look, and we often want others to notice. When a friend compliments my style, it boosts my confidence. If a coworker or neighbor mentions my appearance in a positive way, it feels good. And I am not alone. It satisfies a need within us to be noticed as physically beautiful. We must, however, keep a balance between our desire to please others in our appearance and the need to be identified as beautiful.

To be looked at or treated as physically beautiful by the opposite sex meets deep physical and emotional needs within us. As women, we want to be able to draw the attention and affection of men, whether we are just friends, dating, or married. When a woman dresses to impress a man, she is more likely to select clothes that look sexually appealing so that his attention will be on her. Getting and keeping the attention of men can become a competition among women. It's a game we play by using our physical bodies. The goal is to be more appealing than the other ladies to get more attention. The media shows us how to dress this way, feeding us images of skin-revealing fashion and developing a grip on our minds from an early age. Preteen girls see it in television and movies, teenagers have fashion magazines, and adult women see it in advertising.

What we see has the power to create in our minds an image of ourselves. Women of all ages, including girls in their preteens, have an ideal image in mind. Fashion, popularity, and attention from the opposite sex form a distinct perspective on how we want to look. We begin to tie these three together as early as elementary school. In a study of elementary girls, 72 percent of the girls reported that a sexier outfit related to higher popularity, and 68 percent of the girls would choose to look like the sexy girl over the modern yet less revealing girl.[1] Researchers did note other factors in the decisions, including a girl's exposure to media, the religiousness of the mother, and the mother's self-confidence behaviors.

Image-driven media has had a substantial influence on what we as women think is attractive, acceptable, and downright atrocious. From appropriately behaved princesses to scantily dressed dolls with bad attitudes, the slant toward attractiveness has flooded our image-saturated minds. What we believe to be acceptable, fashionable, and attractive to the opposite sex and to the others we encounter is based mainly on what we see in the world around us.

As a result, we become a walking billboard. How we act and how we dress are a reflection of how we interpret our world. The things we find acceptable and beautiful are the things we choose to wear. Our beliefs and priorities are lived out in our actions. We advertise who we are and what we stand for by the way we look. If we dress in a way that resembles a certain role, we are opening ourselves to playing that part. Think of how Tamar disguised herself as a prostitute (Gen. 38). She removed her mourning robes and veiled her face, allowing herself to shed the identity of a mourner and play the part of a completely different woman. Judah, her own father-in-law, believed the image without recognizing her. She looked the part, so she was able to play the part.

In a similar way, think about modern-day royalty. Perhaps it is a result of the ever-lurking paparazzi, but the royal family of England makes a very elegant and proper statement by the way they dress. The styles Queen Elizabeth II and Duchess Kate choose to wear are often emulated by women who want to be respected. Their styles are considered elegant and represent a manner of behavior that is viewed as sophisticated. Sure, people are drawn to the beauty in the clothing itself, but the clothing also represents the attitudes and conduct of refined and beautiful women. Their clothing sets the stage for their behavior as members of the royal family. The clothes and behaviors are deeply intertwined. As such, these women set an example of beauty, in both their dress and actions, for people around the world.

If we play a part in the image, we also play a role in the actions supporting that image. Dressing and acting in a way that does not represent our true self can be harmful. It can hurt us mentally and emotionally, but it can hurt others too. When we choose to dress and act in a way that represents our identity, we display the beauty that is in us. We become living examples of creation. And in turn, our actions follow. We behave in a way that represents the God who created us beautifully.

The Cost of Beauty

The desire to be physically attractive and outwardly beautiful is costly. According to Forbes.com, in 2015 the average household spent $1,700 a year on clothing, causing the apparel industry to net $12 billion.[2] The average woman has thirty outfits on hand, yet we add to and remove from the collection regularly. As trends change, we crave new because new is what is beautiful. New outfits. New accessories. New shoes. As we change one piece at a time, we transform beauty. The image created by the world of new becomes the definition of beautiful, and we continue to buy it.

But the cost of beauty doesn't stop at fashionable clothing. The many aisles of our local grocery and drug stores are lined with skin cleansers, face masks, hair care, makeup, and other products that promise us "blemish-free," "long-lasting," and "flawless" coverage. The pressure to always *look* beautiful costs an estimated $33 billion each year in the United States. We continue to believe our hair must be the perfect color, our nails must always be painted to match our outfit, and our skin must be blemish-free and silky smooth. We buy product after product to match an image. Many of us are scrubbing away at our self-image in hopes of finding a better reflection of beauty.

Our skewed image of beauty is costing us more than money. The effort and dollars we put into products takes a toll on us physically and emotionally. I look at the number of outfits in my closet and the stacks of daily products on my shelf and see all the ways they didn't work. My failed attempts to fix myself become a reflection on me more than on the product I am using. When I am not blemish free or a perfect fit, I feel ugly. The toll on my mental and emotional self leaves me with a low self-worth. A costly product that does not leave me feeling beautiful becomes an emotional source of feeling like I am not enough.

A Filter for Our Eyes

Look in the mirror. What are the first three things you notice? The chances are good that you picked three things you would change. We identify quickly with our flaws. Our nose that is too wide. The short lashes. The blemish under our lip. We see the things we want to change well before we see what we want to keep. We first see things that fall short of our standards instead of the image of beauty reflected. It is easier to find what does not fit in our definition of beautiful than to identify what does.

Go ahead and look again, this time finding three physical attributes you find beautiful about yourself.

Did it take you a while? You're not alone! It is so easy for us to take one look and find the things we don't like. We can find things that go against our worldly definition of beauty. Trying to flip things around and see qualities in our own reflection that we consider beautiful is difficult. Our minds have been trained this way. We look for beauty by looking for perfection. Our clothes, skin, hair, nails, and more must be absolutely picture perfect before we can call it beautiful. Every detail must be defined and every blemish gone. We lack satisfaction with any detail when one thing falls short of our standard.

Now picture your best girlfriend. What three things do you find physically beautiful about her? Beautiful eyes, incredible hair, or unblemished skin? Our friends are beautiful to us in ways that are easy to define. She has gorgeous hair. Her eyes sparkle. Her smile is eye-catching. We tend to see beauty in others easily but often overlook their imperfections. Does she have wrinkles and laugh lines? Were her nails perfectly painted last week when you met for coffee? Are her roots fading? My guess is that you and I cannot answer these questions with ease unless she happens to be sitting beside us. Your best friend is beautiful to you in physical and emotional ways, just as you are to her.

The beauty developed in the circle of the fashion industry can rob from us the beauty created in relationships. We define beautiful as a style more than a presence. It's what we wear in color and design more than the beauty created in us. Appearance becomes a greater beauty than form and figure. When we hold fast to the idea of beauty as cover-worthy, we place a filter on our eyes. Beautiful becomes comparative. I need to be more beautiful than the other women at work. I need new clothes because her outfits are more flattering than mine. Instead of finding the beauty in what we have, we create a false need for more or better. If we continue to cling to the image of beauty on the surface, we will never find satisfaction. We will continue to buy and buy and buy, but never feel beautiful.

Our eyes have been trained to see our own beauty in the social constructs of the fashion industry. It's magazine models, actresses, and social media icons. Materialistic trends and the "almighty" dollar dictate our conceptions of beauty in our media-savvy world. What we see on Pinterest or YouTube becomes our aim, and we lose sight of the beauty God gave each of us. But beauty is beyond what we put on. Beauty is God-given, not store-bought. It is not a manner of comparing, but a gift uniquely bestowed on each of us.

How do we get beyond our own eyes that so often see our reflection as less than beautiful? How do we see our everyday self as the beautiful creation he has made? It starts with defining beauty from God's point of view.

The Art of Attraction: The Beauty of a Woman

When God created the world, he saw that it was good. The word *good* used in the creation story of Genesis is the Hebrew word *towb.* Used 597 times in the Old Testament, it is translated as *beautiful* in other places in the Bible. Its use here in creation suggests beauty is part of the design of our world. Everything made has an element of beauty. God created beauty when he created the world. It is built-in. It is for everyone to see, and everyone to possess.

By building beauty into creation, God eliminated the need for add-ons. There is nothing we can put on or add to result in more beauty. It's already there. We need to care for it and nurture it. We can enhance it and adorn it, but it has been there since the beginning. God didn't create the fantastic peaks of the mountains only to decide they cannot be beautiful unless covered in snow. The beauty of the mountain is enhanced by the beauty of the snow, but it remains beautiful with or without snow. All of his creation is unique and beautiful in its own way. Each element is different. Different parts of creation complement each other, but each has a beauty of its own.

If beauty is a part of our creation, it is a part of the fabric from which we are made. We do not need to do anything to our bodies to have it. We can't make ourselves beautiful by the way we style our hair or the clothes we wear. Our jewelry, our makeup, and the shape of our body play no part in our natural, God-given beauty. This is what Peter is reminding us of in 1 Peter 3:3, when he says, "Your beauty should not come from outward adornment, such as elaborate hairstyles and the wearing of gold jewelry or fine clothes." Beauty is not what we add to our outward appearance. It cannot be put on.

Peter goes on in verse 4 to explain what will enhance our beauty. He tells us it is the inner qualities of an unchanging gentle and quiet spirit that provides evidence of a woman's beauty. The word *gentle* in this verse is the Greek word *praÿs*. Matthew uses the same word in his Gospel account. Translated there as meekness, *praÿs* refers to the patience and humbleness of a person. The woman who is peaceful, who puts others before herself, and who submits to the godly way of life will show the beauty dwelling inside. It's her expectancy that God is more than herself that makes her beautiful.

Peter describes Abraham's wife, Sarah, as a woman who exhibits this type of beauty. Sarah obediently submitted to Abraham. She peacefully left home to follow God. She agreed to Abraham's instruction to be called his sister when they went to Pharaoh's courts. She stood by as Abraham took Isaac to be sacrificed. Was Sarah perfect in each of these moments? Certainly not! But Abraham was also far from perfect. Obviously, he wasn't trusting God when he agreed with Sarah's plan to have children through Hagar. Both of them muddled through moments like these, and we know they didn't always make godly decisions. We don't either. Yet Sarah is the one Peter chose as an example of beauty because, despite her mistakes, she represents a beauty God desires. A beauty that is evident in her submission. Sure, it may have taken some convincing before she accepted a few things. And as a wife and mother, I can only imagine the arguments Sarah may have had with Abraham. But in the end, she did what was necessary. Her beauty shines in the moments she surrendered her will to what God had planned.

In Genesis, Sarah is described as beautiful using the Hebrew word *yapheh*. Often used to describe the stature or appearance of a person, it is no doubt Sarah was physically beautiful. Her beauty earned her the attention of Pharaoh and others. But Peter's illustration in his letter is not about Sarah's physical appearance: "For *this is the way* the holy women of the past who put their hope in God used to adorn themselves. They submitted themselves to their husbands, like Sarah, who obeyed Abraham and called him her lord" (1 Pet. 3:5—emphasis mine). It is not the way Sarah stood or dressed, but instead it's how she put her hope in God that makes her beautiful to the church.

As women of the church, we are daughters of Sarah. She is an example to us, just as any mother is an example to a daughter. Sarah helps us mold our godly womanhood if we follow in her footsteps. Peter finishes his instructions on the beauty of a woman by highlighting the traits we can take from Sarah: do what is right and do not give way to fear. We are beautiful like Sarah when we are peaceable, humble, and obedient. We are beautiful when we trust in the unfailing love of our God.

When we look at God's Word for instructions on how to be a woman, one key passage is our go-to point on modesty. Paul writes in 1 Timothy 2:9–10, "I also want the women to dress modestly, with decency and propriety, adorning themselves, not with elaborate hairstyles or gold or pearls or expensive clothes, but with good deeds, appropriate for women who profess to worship God." Some arguments are made about the meaning of this verse. Is Paul talking about our clothing or our actions? Are women supposed to be frumpy and makeup-free? And do women have to earn salvation by good works?

No, Paul is not lavishing a lengthy list of rules or imposing works-based salvation on women. If we look at the context and text of this passage, we will find a solid definition of the modesty of a Biblical woman.

What Paul is asking the women of the church to be is modest. Be proper in your circumstances and your appearance. He is not asking us to pretend that beauty and desire do not exist but to acknowledge them as gifts. Use them not to draw attention to yourself, but to glorify the God who gave them to you.

Bathsheba and Esther are two more biblical women commonly known to be beautiful. Described using the Hebrew word *towb*, these women share the same beauty or good used in creation. The earth was created beautiful, as were Bathsheba and Esther. Bathsheba's beauty was noticed from afar and earned her the love of King David. She became his wife, allowing the line of David to continue as a lineage to God's own Son. The beauty of Esther established her as King Xerxes's choice of wife, putting her in a position to save the Jewish people from the government's decrees. The beauty reflected through each of these women allowed God to shine. At the creation of each of these women, God implanted the very same beauty as in the creation of the world.

I Am Beautiful

We have access to the same beauty inside each of us. It is woven into the fabric of our creation. It is when we are broken but relying on the unfailing love of God the beauty shines through. It is when we seek him first and walk in his way that the beauty of our creation is on display for all to see. To feel beautiful is a challenge. We know our creator designs us with beauty inside, and we know it shines through when we walk humbly with God. But how do we stop living in comparison to the clothing racks and magazine ads and to each other?

You are given the ultimate beauty from the beginning. God created you with *your* eyes, with *your* skin, and with *your* hair. He put you together piece by piece. And not only did he craft you as a baby, but he has aged you to the person you are today. Every zit, every wrinkle, and every hair. Being made in his image and by his hand, he looks at you and calls out: beautiful and flawless. He sees the reflection in your eyes and stares in awe of you. He is so in love with you and desires you in every way. And he wants you to see yourself that way!

Look in that mirror one more time and imagine what God sees. The tenderness of your skin. The richness of your eyes. The passion and joy in your smile. His child.

Your beauty is not a reflection that comes from a mirror, but rather a reflection of the God in whose image you are created. It's hard to look in the mirror and see the image God wants us to see. Our humanness hides the beauty with shame and sorrow. Eve's attempt to see things as God sees them resulted in sin, and therefore each of us has lost the sight of real beauty. Have you heard the expression "beauty is from within"? Often we say it to boost the mood of someone who is feeling down about her outward appearance. While well-intended, this statement is often received as a confirmation of a lack of physical beauty. But remember this: beauty, even physical beauty, reflects what is within. We reflect what is living and active on the inside to the outside world. Beauty starts inside.

If you allow Jesus to work in you as you work to follow him, you will reflect an incomparable beauty inside and out. Taking in God's Word and allowing it to feed your soul will help you see life from his perspective. Reading and understanding that your body is the dwelling place of the Spirit will change your perspective, and it becomes easier to treat your body as a temple. You will feed it properly, respect its life, and dress it to represent what is on the inside.

The reflection of a life lived God's way is a beauty untouched by the fashion industry. Beauty becomes more than the way you dress or style your hair, a radiant lifestyle. When your heart is on a beautiful track, your life will be, too. Then you can carry your inner beauty outwardly so that when people look at you, they see your physical beauty as his reflection.

It is okay to feel physically beautiful. The Bible's instructions are not to *not* do your hair and makeup. If those were Peter's instructions, we would have to include on the list to not put on clothes. Rather, we must take the perspective that our outfits and makeup should be more like the snow on the mountains: an add-on that can enhance the natural beauty of our creation. If we are modest in appearance and behavior, we will attract attention in all the right ways. We will draw people into the God who loves them. We will find relationships that satisfy. We will have dignity and feel beautiful beyond what we can measure. And we will have a safe place for the intimacy God has reserved for us.

Shame, fear, and hiding are not what God wants of us. He designed our bodies and created the desires within us. We are not to use our bodies, our clothing, and our sex appeal as weapons against one another but as keys to intimacy and relationships fulfilled in God's way. When our bodies are not a distraction, we are living a life of modesty and propriety. A proper self.

We must act responsibly with our bodies. If we are a living temple of the Holy Spirit, we need to care for our bodies as if they belong to God. We keep them healthy, we keep them in shape, and we keep them clean. We dress them appropriately and polish them up to look our best—all of which require us to spend both time and money in the aisle of beauty products.

Beauty is in us. It is part of who we are in Christ, a piece of our identity. To be beautiful as intended is to live a life reflecting the God who created you as beautiful. Our identity goes beyond the beauty of the retail circle. We are not to live by the world's definition of beautiful but by the beauty of his creation woven into each and every one of us.

I think back to the day of the women's conference when I was called beautiful. Sure, I was dressed well and had put on my best makeup. But I am convinced the beauty that shone in me was obedience. I was nervous about attending alone but did so anyway. My heart was set on God that weekend, and because of my trust in him, I reflected the beauty of God's creation. I truly was beautiful.

Living a Beautiful Life

How does it look to live a life of beauty? It's a life of reflection. We must be mirrors of God, always living in his instruction. Seek out who God is and who he made you to be. Here is how you can practice living a life of beauty:

- **Stop the comparison.** Beauty is not defined by what looks better on her than on you. Every human body and every face is made in his image. Not one is better than the other. The beauty built in our creation is unique and different, but it's always a reflection of God.
- **Be a reflection.** Our most beautiful moments are when we are a mirror. When people see Christ in us, they see the ultimate beauty of all of creation. And that beauty surpasses any creams or make-ups you find in the drugstore aisle.
- **Fill your heart.** If we want to be mirrors of Christ, we must know him intimately. We must fill our hearts and our spirits with his Word. Walking confidently as a reflection means we must have it in our hearts who God is and what he is all about.
- **Walk confidently in your own skin.** Know without a doubt that God made your every detail. He knit you together the way he intended. He doesn't make mistakes, and he has a purpose for everything. Be confident in every good and every flaw, knowing God sees you as his beautiful daughter.

Discussion Questions

1. Tell about a time you felt beautiful.
2. What fashion trends have you loved? What trends have you disliked? What fashion items have you purchased because of a trend, even though you weren't really a fan of them?
3. Discuss the activity of looking in the mirror. What did you see as your good features? What would you change and why?
4. Think about your best girlfriends. Why do you find them beautiful?
5. If your body is the temple in which the Holy Spirit dwells, what can you do to take better care of it? How does this idea change your perspective on your physical body?
6. Look at the original biblical writings about Sarah (Sarai), Esther, Bathsheba, and Rebecca. Talk about their physical beauty, as well as their created beauty.
7. Creation is designed to enhance the beauty in each other. If our beauty pours out of our gentle and humble spirit, how can we enhance the beauty of each other? What can you do to change the definition of beautiful in your circle of influence?
8. How can you put into practice the things Sarah taught us were beautiful? List three things you can do to live out the example set by Sarah.

9. Write a prayer to thank God for a time when you felt his beauty shining through you. Ask him to shine the beauty inside you outwardly as you seek him fully.

NOTES

[1]Christine R. Starr and Gail M. Ferguson, "Sexy Dolls, Sexy Grade-Schoolers? Media and Maternal Influences on Young Girls' Self-Sexualization," *Sex Roles* 67 (October 2012): 463. https://doi.org/10.1007/s11199-012-0183-x.

[2]Emma Johnson, "The Real Cost of Your Shopping Habits," accessed June 21, 2018, https://www.forbes.com/sites/emmajohnson/2015/01/15/the-real-cost-of-your-shopping-habits/#4545b1bf1452.

Thoughts and Reflections

3

Successful

Successful (adj): resulting or terminating in success.

College is said to be the best years of your life. You can be independent and free. Students make their own choices and gain experience in the real world over the safety net of structured courses. Adults become coaches more than disciplinarians, and the future is up to the student. It's the first step into adulthood.

College was not the best time of my life, as I thought it should be. I spent a lot of time wandering and wondering what direction I wanted to go for the rest of my life. My first steps into adulthood looked more like slowly climbing the hill of a roller coaster than the wild ride I thought they would be. My high school friends had big plans postgraduation. Most of them knew where they were going to college and what they were going to study. They were career-oriented with a plan for the future. Not me. I had no idea what I wanted to be when I grew up. The hill others climbed in high school let them zoom through college with all its twists, turns, and loops. For me, I climbed the hill blindly, wondering what course would be set before me.

I had good grades in high school and did well on my college entrance exams. My parents typically heard good things from my teachers throughout my school years, and I was rarely in trouble. I was your typical smart but shy kid. I followed the status quo, doing whatever was expected of me. I may not have ranked in the top ten, or even the top 10 percent, but I had good grades. People often told me I had a bright future, but I had no idea what to do with it. I went to college because it was the logical thing for a smart girl to do, but I had no personal motivation to be there.

I can clearly remember my first semester of college. The campus was just thirty minutes from home, but it was worlds out of my comfort zone. I entered as a science major with a love for children and research. I hoped somewhere along the way the two would merge, but I arrived with no clue how that would happen. I moved to campus in the fall with zero ambition. I didn't know what to do.

Through the course of my college career, I changed majors three times. In doing so, I was exposed to many classes, professors, and topics. I had courses in the medical sciences, in history, educational psychology, business, economics, accounting, nutrition, and sports psychology. I even had the chance to take art classes like photography and pottery, and physical fitness classes like swimming and broomball. In all the variety of classes, I did well. I achieved mostly good grades. But I still had no plans for my future. Every class led to more confusion than clarity. To what field was I genuinely gifted if I could be smart in all of them?

I was nearing the end of my time after spending my final two years working toward a degree in health and sports. I inquired of my professors about a professional certification that often followed the degree and typically set people on a career path. The certification required you to pass a very large exam and offered professional credentials to those who passed. Letters after your name had to mean you were smart.

One afternoon, a particular professor pulled me aside and told me I would never pass this exam. He assured me I was not going to amount to anything. The words cut into my soul. For four and a half years, I had worked hard to earn good grades in everything, and now this man stood before me deeming me a flop. I had the academic status to be considered smart, but I lacked the capability. His commentary applied to the field of public health, but in my mind, I expanded it to all of life. His words made me believe I would never make it outside the classroom.

I chose to take the test, despite my lowered level of confidence. I felt the need to prove that I was smart. I wanted to prove my challenging professor wrong. To be able to say, "I am certified." I graduated a few weeks later, and I received the results. I had passed the test. I had proved, once again, that I had the academic knowledge to succeed. But somehow my excitement was lacking . . . the letters after my name felt empty. I still didn't feel any more capable than I did after my conversation with the skeptical professor. I continued to believe his words.

I aimed to be smart for so many years. I wanted to get good grades and do math problems at the kitchen table with my dad. I tried to spell correctly and type at lightning fast speeds like my mom. I wanted to be part of the smart group of students at school. I equated being smart with accomplishment. Good grades get you into college. College gets you a respectable job. And a decent job gets you a career and a family.

Smart was my life plan. It would guide me through all my dreams. To be smart led one to be successful. An academic career of good grades and a college degree was supposed to earn me a fast track to success. Instead, it left me in a confused mess, wondering how I could be smart and unsuccessful at the same time.

Straight A Student

Success is a word tossed around as motivation for students; it's talked about as if it were the end goal. Success can be achieved, but it is rarely attained without effort. To be successful in our world is to arrive. To have reached the end with something to show for all our work.

Early in life, success is based on our academic performance. We are taught from a young age to be good in school. Work hard and get an A. For many of us, doing well in school made the adults in our lives proud. Struggling caused them to think less of us. Grades often led to rewards and punishments. Teachers often rewarded top scores, inadvertently showing their disappointment with the struggling kids. Parents tell friends and family about straight As, but they often take away leisure activities such as social time and screen time for lower scores. Even peers find out about the scores of others when things like group projects and significant tests come around. We quickly learn the positive and negative reinforcements associated with our performance in the classroom.

In the early years of school, girls are often praised heavily for their knowledge, while boys receive praise for appropriate behavior. This is the foundation for a young girl's need to do well academically. As we grow, people give praise that connects the idea of smart with academic performance. Many people would agree that good grades indicate a higher level of intelligence, but studies in education and psychology show that academic performance is only loosely correlated to intelligence. Grades are often indicators of proper organization, self-discipline, and the ability to do what is expected. Standardized tests are better measures of intelligence.

However, neither intelligence nor grades are predictors of success beyond the classroom. In fact, one researcher followed high school valedictorians and salutatorians into college and the workforce. While most of them finished college and often went on to earn graduate degrees, they did not find a spot toward the top of their respective fields. In other words, they typically are not visionaries and world-changers. They are hard workers who do well at their upper-class jobs.[1]

Beyond our actual skills, our elementary years are formational in how we interpret our ability. By fifth grade, boys and girls typically have an equal academic ability. When presented with a challenge, girls are more likely to give up merely because they perceive the work as beyond their capacity.[2] Girls will limit their efforts because they think they should understand easily. We believe what we know is what we know, and that our ability to understand is unchangeable. We doubt ourselves. We give up. We think if we don't get it the first time, we never will. Boys, on the other hand, look at the difficult material as a challenge. It is often motivating and challenging to learn something new. Beginning in the formative age, the male brain accepts learning as a gain and will pursue new things with higher motivation.

Women are on the move upward in the workforce, requiring a demand for intelligence across many platforms. As a result, girls are digging deep into their academic careers. On average, girls will graduate high school with a higher GPA than boys. In 2015, women earned nearly 60 percent of all bachelor's degrees and almost 60 percent of all master's degrees.[3] We read more, we talk more, and we typically do better in school than boys.

This pattern of thinking about challenges continues into adulthood. Women will often doubt their intelligence because they perceive their knowledge as capped. What we know is what we know, and we can't change it or add to it. We operate on the belief that we cannot learn anything new. We deem our success to be at its maximum.

Believing we already know everything that we can possibly know damages our ability to keep trying. When we feel as if we are the most successful we will ever be, we stop trying to be better. We often set up camp in this place we believe to be the mountain peak of our knowledge. It becomes a cap on our achievable success. We move on from our education, thinking what we know is all we will ever need. We search for a place in the workforce where we are on the top of our game. We expect immediate success for all the time and effort we put into our academic endeavors.

For some of us, our academic achievements seem to have left us on the hilltop. We look down and see the effort we put in to climb this high, and we believe we have reached the top. We accept the idea that this is as high as we can go. Despite our best efforts, we could not attain the status of "smart" and therefore seek low-level jobs. We believe that our lesser education has permanently capped our success in the workplace. But academic success is not a precursor to workforce success. If we see our campsite as a temporary home in the middle of the climb, we gain the perspective needed to keep moving. We reach beyond the perceived cap to continue learning, growing, and developing. This process opens new doors to success in the workplace.

Success is often tied to a career. Doctors and lawyers tend to have reached success when they are able to work in a steady practice. Athletes reach success when they have a winning season or win a championship. Salesmen reach success when they make a sales quota, teachers when their students pass standardized tests, and mechanics when they get a car to run. A successful career has a positive result.

Success in the workplace seems to be found in the achievement of something tangible. Sometimes it's an outcome, and sometimes it's a job title. In June of 2017, Fortune 500 announced a record high that thirty-two of its companies boasted female CEOs.[4] That's 6.4 percent. Eleven of the thirty-two were named CEO in 2016. Mary Barra, the first female CEO in the automobile industry, has earned General Motors a top-ten spot since taking on the role in 2015.

The 115th Congress of the United States (2017–2019) included 105 women. That's just shy of 20 percent. The same Congress brought the first birth by an active senator in 2018 when Tammi Duckworth delivered her baby in late April of 2018. Of the nine justices in the Supreme Court, a woman has held at least one seat since the nomination of Sandra Day O'Connor in 1981. And five members of President Donald Trump's first-term cabinet were female, including the first-ever mom to be the press secretary.

The Department of Labor's 2010 report estimates more than 60 percent of women work outside the home, totaling nearly 47 percent of the total labor force in the United States. In the 1960s, only 38 percent of women worked outside the home. Today, women make up a sizable portion of the job market requiring additional degrees and studies. Nearly 34 percent of doctors, 35 percent of lawyers, and 76 percent of teachers are women with professional degrees. Women have expanded into careers like police officers (13 percent), firefighters (7 percent), and construction workers (26 percent), using knowledge and skills previously thought to be male-oriented.

If we base our view of success on our position in the workforce, what becomes of the stay-at-home mom? When a woman is asked about her occupation, a stay-at-home mom will often reply with something like, "I'm just a mom." The shyness or reservation in her thoughts is often carried outwardly in her tone of voice. She is often labeled as "less than" because she is perceived as a woman who sits at home all day. The job of mom does not come with an income or an office. It doesn't offer healthcare, paid vacation, or a yearly bonus. Instead, it is full of mundane tasks. It's tedious, repetitive, and tiring. With endless piles of laundry, it is easy to feel like you are going nowhere. The repetitive cycles of the job can feel unsuccessful and lonely.

Women who choose to be stay-at-home moms or stay-at-home wives are certainly not unsuccessful. Despite the perceived lack of appreciation, 60 percent of Americans believe it is important to have a parent home with the children in their formative years.[5] Some researchers have even found a correlation between academic success from the early years to high school and the amount of time spent with a parent. Other benefits of stay-at-home parenting include decreased family spending, quality of family time, and increased opportunities for volunteer work.[6] Success for the stay-at-home mom sits below the standard of worldly success, leaving many to struggle with their feelings and decisions.

The struggle to feel successful for a stay-at-home mom is similar to the struggle to feel successful as a working woman. In all situations, the expectations for success can seem pretty high. Those who meet the requirements are typically rewarded handsomely. Recognitions and awards are handed out for highest successes. Fancy cars, elaborate houses, and designer handbags become the trophies we carry. Mary Kay offers a pink Cadillac to its consultants who gross more than $100,000 in revenue within a year. Realtors often award vacations to their top salespeople. One bank in the Pacific Northwest reportedly offers a clothing allowance for their new employees to purchase top-notch clothing in order to keep the name of the bank polished and upscale. The tangible feel of success soon becomes the definition for many of us. Without the trophies and luxuries, we begin to feel less than enough.

In this way, success begins to look a lot like perfection. We begin to cling to the same standards where successful becomes perfect, lacking in nothing. To be successful in my class, I must get an A. To be successful in my college career, I need to have a 4.0 grade point average. To be successful in my job, I need to be the highest grossing salesperson. The standards of success become as unachievable as perfection. A difficult paper, a sick day from work, or a less-than-average standardized test score keeps me from perfection and gives me the dissatisfaction of being unsuccessful.

If we allow ourselves to cling to a definition of success as having the top spot in the company or the top grade in the class, we begin to feel less valuable when we miss those marks. The need to parade around with our worldly trophies and impress others by our job well done drives us to continue reaching. When we miss the mark, even slightly, we often lose our focus on the job and look only for the rewards. We crave the pats on the back, the "my daughter" brags, and the attention of the crowds. We fix our eyes on the prizes—big and small—and forget about the task at hand. Our reach for success limits our grip on God's plan in our life.

Achieving More: Wisdom Is Success

The idea of success is broad-ranging, from prosperous to wise to right. The English language defines *success* as a favorable or desired outcome. It is found twenty-six times in the New International Version of the Bible, all of which occur in the Old Testament. Six unique Hebrew words are translated as success, giving us as broad-ranging a meaning for the word in the Bible as it has in English.

The two words most commonly translated as success are also translated as prosper. The Hebrew word *tsalach* is used forty-four times in the NIV as prosper or prosperous. It is used to discuss a positive result or gain. Joseph was known to be prosperous for his good works in Egypt. David is said to be prosperous from his anointing and throughout his reign. This use of the Hebrew is the same as our English use for the idea of material success.

The Hebrew word *sakal* is also commonly translated as prosper. More often this word is translated as understanding. To be successful, therefore, is to have a good understanding or to be wise about something. The word *sakal* is also translated as wise or wisdom. This type of wisdom is what Eve sought when she ate the fruit. "When the woman saw that the fruit of the tree was good for food and pleasing to the eye, and also desirable for gaining wisdom [*sakal*], she took some and ate it" (Gen. 3:6a—emphasis mine). Eve desired the wisdom to know what was good and what was not. She wanted to achieve the highest level of understanding she could. She wanted to be successful.

To be successful in Biblical usage is to be wise and prosperous. Solomon is known to have been very wise and prosperous. He asked God for wisdom, and he developed into one of the greatest kings in biblical history. He built temples and ships, acquired land and goods, established trades and offerings, and did other prosperous things. God blessed his work and his worship, promising to keep his descendants on the throne for as long as they followed him faithfully with integrity and uprightness (1 Kings 9:4). The most significant thing about King Solomon is this: "King Solomon was greater in *riches and wisdom* than all the other kings of the earth. The whole world sought audience with Solomon to hear the wisdom God had put in his heart" (1 Kings 10:23–24—emphasis mine). Solomon had it all—the riches, the temples, the armor. Yet he used his wisdom to teach others. He used his renown to share about the God he followed. He was an influencer, and he used his passion for faithfully following God and influencing others.

Despite his world renown and wisdom, Solomon lacked a significant amount of understanding about success. In his quest to gain success, he lost something important. He allowed his popularity and riches to become stumbling blocks to his home life. He set his eyes on influencing the world around him but missed the chance to influence his descendants and the generations to come to live in godly ways. His need for worldly success clouded his ability to pass along the legacy of faith.

How do we gain the wisdom of Solomon so that we can be influencers both at home and beyond? We put aside our need to have complete head-knowledge of God, and we begin to grow our heart-knowledge. It is not what we know because we researched it, but it is what we know because he said it. If you want instruction on wisdom, how to get it, and what power it has for God's people, turn to the book of Proverbs. Proverbs 9:10 tells us that the beginning of wisdom is reverence to God. When we develop a relationship of respect for the Lord, we have the beginnings of wisdom. We must position ourselves to gain his wisdom so that it reaches beyond our heads and penetrates our hearts. It may come at a cost. We must give of ourselves to gain of him. It is a continual process with no endpoint. We are not to stop listening and searching. We cannot let ourselves forget what has been poured into our hearts by the giver of wisdom.

If we position ourselves to receive God's wisdom, we have God's promises of protection. Proverbs 4:6 tells us wisdom will protect us and watch over us. Proverbs 9:11 says through wisdom our days will be many and years will be added to our life. Wisdom is a precious gift that will walk with us through challenges and moments of despair. It will help us in good times when we can speak to others. Jesus even promised to give us the words and wisdom to contradict anyone who puts us on trial for our beliefs, if we open our minds and our mouths to his guidance (Luke 21:15).

How do we know if we have gained wisdom? James poses this same question in his letter recorded in the New Testament as the book of James. He explains that the wise will show their wisdom through the life they lead. "Who among you is wise? Let them show it by their good life, by deeds done in humility that comes from wisdom" (James 3:13). When we act with a humble heart and do good deeds with no expectations, we are acting in wisdom. James continues by telling us that wisdom from heaven is pure. It is peaceful, considerate, submissive, full of mercy, impartial, and sincere. If you are acting with your heart knowledge, your words and your actions will follow suit. It's not the trophies we tote around with us; it's the attitude with which we live our lives.

Wisdom is a gift given by God who is infinitely wise. He allows us to gain wisdom when we passionately seek him in words and actions. We are not required to memorize a certain number of Bible verses, but to continually read our Bibles in search of wisdom. Head knowledge is good and useful, but with God, continual pursuit of heart knowledge is preferred. "For the mouth speaks what the heart is full of" (Luke 6:45).

I Am Successful

The best learners seek knowledge by following a passion. If you are highly interested in something, you will continue to study it until you understand. The same is true for those who pursue wisdom. James 1:5 tells us to ask God for wisdom when we lack, and he will give it to us generously. He follows that promise by reminding us we must honestly believe God will provide, but not to expect to receive anything. We ask God for it, but we must pursue it with passion, not expecting it to fall into our lap.

Success in God's world is not gained by being the best performer or highest achiever. It has nothing to do with your salary, what kind of clothes you wear, or your IQ. Success as God designed it is the wisdom and prosperity brought on by your faithfulness. It's a passionate pursuit of him. Listen to me, dear sister: When was the last time you received a grade on your daily life? Did your dinner last night earn you an A? Did your penmanship get you a bonus coupon when you signed for your grocery purchase? Did you get a candy bar for picking up your kids on time?

You are not graded on your ability in life. There is no reward for an A+ in dishes, and no punishment for an F in folding the laundry. It's not about how smart you are in life; it's about using your abilities to fulfill your God-given purpose. It's not about being the best; it's about being wise.

Culture tells us to be smart. Book smart. Street smart. Business smart. Fashion smart. We must be the highest achiever, make the most money, and raise the next generation. The world says we need to do it all to be successful. God says we must ask. We must pursue and follow, not measuring our wisdom in comparison to others.

As women we are influencers. We are the educators, the caregivers, the socialites. Our voices are heard not just in the big picture, but every day by the people who live and work near us. If we are waiting for success, we may be missing opportunities to show others our abilities. We are not required to be the smartest or the highest achieving. Friends and family do not ask for advice or friendship because we graduated twenty-seventh in our class. People come to us because they value our insights, which are rooted in our heart knowledge. We are to pursue wisdom with passion and purpose so that we can pass it along. Success is passionately pursuing God and bringing others along.

It was in college that I was introduced to the God who loves me beyond my own understanding. Perhaps the label of smart that I tried to achieve in the years prior ran me in circles chasing my own tail. My smart had left me feeling lost and unprepared for a future. But God had me exactly where he wanted me to be. I began to pursue him and let his wisdom guide me. Will you, too, surrender to the protection of wisdom instead of the allure of success?

Living a Life of Success

How does it look to live a life of wisdom? It's a life of searching and praying. We continually ask to receive God's wisdom while never stopping the search. Here is how you can practice living a life of wisdom:

- **Study the Word.** Search for relevance and meaning to the world in the Scriptures. Constantly engage in what wisdom the Bible offers.
- **Study the world.** Look at the world God made and search for his answers. Always know what

is going on around you so you can be wise in your responses.

- **Let go of earning credit.** Sometimes you get things right, and sometimes you don't. You are not being graded on performance, so study for wisdom and not just knowledge.
- **Embrace challenge.** When something gets hard, don't assume you can't do it. Take it on as a challenge. Work hard to figure it out.
- **Stretch your mind.** Sometimes we don't get it right. Take a step back and search for answers yourself instead of trusting in what you have been told.

Discussion Questions

1. When did you know what you wanted to do when you "grew up"? Did it come true?
2. Discuss a time when you faced a challenge and wanted to give up. When did you face a challenge, but persevered to finish?
3. If you had to pick one area you feel smart, what would it be? Book smart? Math smart? Fashion smart?
4. What is something you once believed true but later found to be false?
5. Who do you influence?
6. How does your life show the wisdom God has given you?

NOTES

[1]Eric Barker, "Wondering What Happened to Your Class Valedictorian? Not Much, Research Shows," Money (website), *Time*, May 18, 2017, http://time.com/money/4779223/valedictorian-success-research-barking-up-wrong.

[2]Heidi Grant Halvorson, "The Trouble with Bright Girls," The Science of Success (blog), *Psychology Today*, January 27, 2011, https://www.psychologytoday.com/us/blog/the-science-success/201101/the-trouble-bright-girls.

[3]National Center for Education Statistics, January 2017, https://nces.ed.gov/programs/digest/d16/tables/dt16_318.30.asp?current=yes.

[4]Jena McGregor, "The Number of Women CEOs in the Fortune 500 Is at an All-Time High—of 32," On Leadership, *Washington Post*, June 7, 2017, https://www.washingtonpost.com/news/on-leadership/wp/2017/06/07/the-number-of-women-ceos-in-the-fortune-500-is-at-an-all-time-high-of-32/?utm_term=.a3c55addf7b9.

[5]Apryl Duncan, "What Research Says about Being a Stay-at-Home Mom," *Very Well Family*, April 5, 2018, https://www.verywellfamily.com/research-stay-at-home-moms-4047911.

[6]Amy Robleski, "8 Reasons It's Okay to Not Work (Even After Your Kids Start School)," Parents as People, *Parent*, February 1, 2017, http:// www.parent.com/8-reasons-its-okay-to-not-work-even-after-your-kids-start-school.

Thoughts and Reflections

4

Bold

Bold (adj): fearless before danger; showing or requiring a fearless, daring spirit.

One of my favorite childhood movie series is *The Mighty Ducks*. Gordon Bombay and Charlie Conway. The three-part series of movies follows a group of misfit neighborhood kids in suburban Minnesota who play peewee hockey. Coached by a hotshot lawyer whose personal trouble forces him into community service hours, the team transforms from ragamuffins to champions.

In the second movie, the female lead role is that of the now traveling team's tutor. My favorite scene in this second movie is when circumstances force her to coach the team. Having no idea what to do and no confidence to do it, she willingly steps in to care for the kids she has come to love. The players lend a hand to the confused tutor as she grows in confidence through the game. Her newfound confidence is evident in one moment when she must be bold. "Change it up!" she yells, and the team responds. It is a moment of satisfaction, one you can almost feel as you see it on her face. As a young girl watching this scene, even I recognized her boldness. She stepped up to the plate and acted for the people in her life. It was encouraging and exciting, and an introverted girl like me decided I would speak up for those I cared about, too.

Standing up for someone I care about seems easy, but sometimes it's harder than I think it will be. I can't help but think of women like Rachel Scott and Victoria Leigh Soto, who gave up their lives to protect the people they cared about most. Scott was a teenager in 1999 when two high school boys walked into the school and murdered seventeen students and one teacher. She was the first to be shot. She stood in defense of her faith in Christ to the moment of her death. Soto was a first-grade teacher at Sandy Hook Elementary in December 2012. When a gunman entered her school, Soto hid her students in the closet and told the gunman they were in a different room. She was shot and killed moments later, but her students were unharmed because of her bold actions. Dawn Hochsprung, Mary Sherlach, and Anne Marie Murphy were caring staff members of Sandy Hook who gave their lives for the students in the incident that December morning, reportedly holding children in their arms or lunging after the suspect.

Most of us will never be asked to give up our lives for others, but our boldness can be shown in other ways. During one season of life, I had the privilege of substitute teaching. One day, I was standing in front of a classroom of fifth graders when a young boy loudly declared his distaste for the work of a talented young girl who had been called upon to present in front of the class. His snickering and degrading made me alert. I was brought back to a time in my middle school years when I wished a teacher or friend would have stood boldly for me. I decided I wanted this girl to feel what it was like to be protected and appreciated. I refused to let the students criticize the work of their peers in this way. The boy in this class showed boldness by refusing to appreciate others, and I had to be bold to stand against the laughing crowd in support of the girl. My stance may not have been as bold as the women who have come before me, but I hope the girl felt loved and cared for that day and always.

I Say What I Want

From an early age, we are often taught we can be whoever we want to be and do what we want to do. We are challenged to push our limits. Dream big. The sky is the limit on what we can do if we just take a stand for it. This message is intended to be an encouragement to work hard and achieve our dreams, a way of telling us we are unstoppable and full of potential.

But we have stretched this encouraging thought to be permission to live however we choose. We have morphed the idea of being ourselves into an excuse to step on others, be offensive, and be offended. Being an individual of our own creation allows us to pick and choose the rules and morals we want. We begin to think poorly of others who choose to be different from ourselves. Our moral compass points to behaviors as individually acceptable and unacceptable, and these will not always be the same as our neighbor. We offend people in our words and actions. We are easily offended when another's choice looks different from our own. "Be you" has changed from finding your place in society to defining your way over others. The freedom to do, say, and act in any manner we choose has altered our cultural climate. Opinions and beliefs are individualized and frequently verbalized. We open our mouths to express every thought before we consider any other point of view.

We have created a "say what you want" environment. People are speaking up and speaking out more than ever. From real and fake news to argument-inducing tweets, the words we are speaking to one another are changing. Bold has reached beyond standing up for what is morally or socially right. It has become a free-for-all chance to express our opinions. Instead of encouraging young girls to break the molds of gender bias or stereotype to reach for their God-given potential, we are aiding them to express every thought that comes to mind and stand against everything that binds them.

If you need evidence of our uncanny ability to speak out, check Twitter. Countless arguments between celebrities, government officials, and others have become national news. People lash out over appearances, relationships, and political views. Everything from a woman's makeup choice, her clothing, and how she voted in the last election to who she is dating this week becomes a topic of debate. Marked frequently by harsh words, social media is an open-air arena for verbal battle. Some women stand firm against discrimination and sexual harassment, yet turn to the Twitter-verse to rant about a fellow woman. Political arguments regarding public policy have found an outlet in the allotted 140 characters of Twitter. Even those who fight for biblical morals seem to be taken by the ability to use social media to announce and attack the world's issues. It has become a platform for making our views known in many realms of daily life, regardless of morals and offensiveness.

Not unlike Twitter's open door for offensive remarks, activists on all sides have taken to the vocal and visual claims of their views. Many activist communities are using vulgarities and other foul language rants in public to express their beliefs. From the infamous women's movement pink hats to the graphic displays of the pro-choice and anti-abortion movements, we have become a nation of people who speak up whenever something offends us. We quickly point fingers at those who have differing opinions. We exclude others who disagree with our point of view. It becomes a dividing factor, where we are constantly offending others or being offended by others.

With no reservation, people are gathering in numbers to make their claims heard. Local businesses and organizations are being boycotted. Government squares are flooded by protestors. Sit-ins, corner picketers, and street marches are happening regularly. Words oppose words, and images contend with images. It's a battle of wills. Some have turned into screaming matches and fistfights. Others become legal battles. The lines that once defined us as individuals living in a land of independence now break us apart. Hate is common, and division is harsh.

Desire and the lack of grace is crippling our society. Instead of embracing differences and teaching morals, we are casting stones. Tact and human connection are traded for bullhorns and closed ears. The louder the call, the more attention it gets, and in the process, we have lost the mix of grace and truth that results in progress. People in the headlines sometimes seem to be calling for rights to make a point or satisfy a personal desire rather than for the good of the whole. It seems as if some want to be noticed more than they want to make a difference in the community.

To be noticed, women all around are shouting every desire and argument that stirs within. The collective of women shouting with their voices and their lives has cast a shadow, as if they represent the entire female population. To the general population, it seems as if women are coming in full force to make a statement on one side or the other. We pass blame and fight among ourselves. We march around with vulgar words and tasteless images. We forsake privacy and style for volume and attention as we declare our needs. And while many women are minding their own business or hiding from any labels attaching them to this loud campaign, the generalization of bold women has labeled us all.

The feminist movement is an example of this. The boldness of the women's movement has become the voice of anger and uproar for many women. A national survey by the *Washington Post* and Kaiser Family Foundation finds six in ten women and one-third of men call themselves feminist, with roughly seven in ten of each saying the movement is empowering. Yet more than four in ten Americans see the movement as angry, and a similar portion says it unfairly blames men for women's challenges.[1]

Speaking out for or against anything is an immediate invitation to ridicule. Our beliefs may be offensive to another person, creating an environment where everything we say or do is violating someone. We are bombarded with arguments supporting two opposing views, no matter the topic. Yet we are encouraged to speak out against anything and everything we think is wrong. Whether you agree or disagree with the motivating factor as the need to be heard, we can agree our volume is getting louder. We are speaking out now more than ever on all sides of every issue. Our desire to be heard is overshadowing our desire to make changes. We have pushed our right to free speech further than any period of our nation's history. The U.S. Constitution affords Americans the privilege that no law will be made to prohibit free speech. No law or court can keep you and me from saying, writing, or otherwise expressing our opinions, but that does not mean there are no consequences to us. We are divided in our country on many issues, including women's rights, partly because we have been told to be bold with our voices.

We, as followers of Christ, walk with this boldness. We are the ones expressing our opinions on Twitter, marching for rights, and raising our voices for change. Marching in the Right to Life and pro-choice rallies, participating in the Women's March, protesting for or against same-sex marriage and rights regarding sexual orientation, kneeling or standing for the anthem. We are the ones carrying signs: those with messages of love and messages of hate. We are the ones boycotting and protesting. On both sides of every issue, we are among the bold faces and voices shouting out our beliefs. We are an active part of the women of this country.

When to Open, When to Shut

Bold moves have a place in our world. Without bold women, we might not have the right to vote or equal opportunities in school. We must be bold in our faith, too, always acting in a way that is true to the God we follow. At times that will require us to be bold. There are times when we must pull our strength from faith and stand against opposition. When we are called to stand bold, we must remember to do so with grace and poise. It will rarely require us to be loud or point fingers.

Fighting for the rights of citizenship and the right to vote, women gathered together to speak up for women's rights as early as the 1840s. For many years, women gathered to discuss how to go about gaining these rights in a male-dominated society. It took more than seventy years of gatherings by the women of this country for the United States to afford equal rights like voting, representation in government, land-ownership abilities, and educational opportunities. The Nineteenth Amendment provided women the right to vote in 1920. The Civil Rights Act of 1964 extended equal opportunities in schools, workplaces, and public accommodations to all men and women, not dependent on race, color, sex, religion, or country of origin. The inclusion of gender in this set of qualifications seems to have its own story. Some historians feel the reason lawmakers added women to this list was to prevent its passing in a vote. Instead, it did pass with women included among the list of people who had received little acknowledgement from the government and society in that period of history.

The fight for all of these rights was not easy and took many women time and effort. They had to stand against the opposition without fear or finger-pointing. Legally, women were gaining ground through these efforts. Feminists like Betty Friedan, author of the 1963 book *The Feminine Mystique*, continued to gather into organizations supporting the social aspects of being a woman. Fighting for equal job opportunities, equal pay, and equal access to higher education, the women's movement stood for the advancement of all women.

In 1967, Katherine Switzer pushed the limits of inclusion in gentle ways. Since women were restricted from running in national sporting events, she registered for the Boston Marathon using her initials.[2] Switzer started the race beside her coach, only to be physically pushed from the course by officials. Her male companions for the race took a stand with her, and she finished the race despite the negative attention. Switzer did not degrade her fellow racers or the officials. She merely did what she set out to do and found outlets to take a stand for female athletes. She continued to pursue her passion of running even after the public debacle in Boston. Over time, she gathered women runners around the globe, spearheading the petition of the International Olympic Committee to add the women's marathon to its event lineup in the summer games of 1986. Switzer returned to run several Boston Marathons, including the 2017 race, on the fiftieth anniversary of the famed push. At seventy years of age, the anniversary race marked her fortieth marathon completion.

Prior to the Equal Opportunity Act in 1974, a woman—single, widowed, or divorced—would meet resistance if she tried to establish credit in her name. In most cases, she would not be able to open a bank account or credit card without the cosignature of a man. A woman's money was managed by a man, and she had no legal rights to property ownership without him, either. A small percentage of women worked outside the home, but they were likely to lose their jobs when they became pregnant. They were expected to forfeit their workplace for the role of motherhood. Women had to depend heavily on their husbands or fathers for financial security.

In 1973, the landmark Supreme Court decision in the case of *Roe v. Wade*, brought women's reproductive rights to the forefront of social issues. The ruling brought a new sense of privilege to women regarding the ownership of their bodies, including their ability to give life. Abortions became legal. Women were given the green light to manage their bodies in whatever way they saw fit. Rights to education and military work were drawn to the surface, creating rifts between family structure and the working rights of women that still stand in the debate today.

Bold as defined by culture is loud and opinionated. It is the expression "the squeaky wheel gets the grease," lived out in our real-world lives. The misconception that the louder we get, the more attention we receive grows stronger. So we get louder. And our message gets more convoluted and twisted until we no longer look like women fighting for what is right, but instead we look like obnoxious, unaccepting voice boxes fighting to be known.

When we cling to bold as a volume, we lose our audience. Voices are raised, and ears turn off. The more we strengthen our choice of words or images for the impact, the less credible we are seen to be. A screaming woman using profanity and images of abuse loses impact and lessens the likelihood of change. Our ugly side is not going to win the battle. In fact, the harsher we become, the more defensiveness is built on the other side. By being bold in accordance with the world, we begin to look like hypocrites. We lose credibility. Our fight becomes more about winning than about the compassion we have for those for whom we are fighting. When we leave grace behind to be heard, we are jading the beliefs and values in our life. Our boldness cannot make a difference if our morals are compromised.

For Such a Time as This: Bold for a Purpose

A look through the Gospel of John defines the social climate of boldness during Jesus's ministry. Throughout this account, we can see the progression from the boldness of the people to the boldness of Jesus himself. In John 7, the disciples ask Jesus to make a public declaration of his position, but he declines telling them it is not yet time for him to be bold in that way. Many of the religious leaders asked him to declare his identity, hoping to force him into verbally claiming to be God in order to further their case against him. John also tells us of people in the town who were afraid to speak up for fear of the religious leaders. Yet as Jesus's ministry continued, there came a time when Jesus told the disciples he would speak boldly. Jesus knew from the start that there was a right time to speak with boldness.

English translations of the Bible use the words "boldness" and "confidence" for the same Greek word, *parresia.* Defined as "unreserved speech, cheerful courage, and the deportment by which one secures publicity," this word packs a punch. Jesus spoke boldly about his mission, and the disciples carried on the message with a great confidence that gained attention. Several times Paul and other writers of the New Testament speak of bold or confident declarations of God's message of love.

A woman of the Bible well-known for her boldness is Esther. From beginning to end, her story stands as an example of boldness for the greater good. She didn't argue or fight, yet she made a stand for her people and her God.

Esther was a young, beautiful Jewish girl who was living in exile. During the time of exile, it was common for a Jew not to reveal her roots. Being raised by her uncle in a foreign land, she lived as if she belonged there. When King Xerxes began his search for a new queen, he called for all the women in his land to be gathered and brought to his courts. In following the laws decreed, Esther was obedient to her country. She went to the palace, continuing to live as one who belonged rather than an exiled Jew. She did what she was required to do by law. She didn't fight it or ask for extraordinary circumstances. She walked alongside the other women and did what they did. She listened to the advice and instruction of the king's servants and her uncle. She was careful not to break God's law, but she never argued against her king's law either.

Esther found favor with the king's people and with God. The servant in charge of the queening process found her to be special and expedited her beauty treatments. She stood out as remarkable. The servant provided her with all the things she needed and offered her advice on how to win the king's affection. Esther did not challenge or argue with him. She respected her role and by doing so gained the help of people closest to the king. Then the king himself found her beautiful and loved her. She continued to be obedient and to do what was asked of her even after being chosen as queen. She served as queen for more than five years before she had to choose between her king and her people.

When a decree was issued to remove the exiles from the land, Esther was forced to act boldly. Knowing the kingdom's rules for standing before the king uninvited, she had to choose between respecting the king and saving her people. She fasted and prayed, preparing herself for God to do what was necessary. And when the time was right, Esther had to choose to act respectfully in the face of danger. Esther didn't make demands of the king or try to change the law herself. She didn't convince others to cause an uproar with her. She gracefully yet boldly made her move without fear of the harsh repercussions. The king offered her the scepter as a sign of invitation because she had won his respect. He honored her choice and listened to her concerns. She revealed to him her heritage and the effects of his decree on her people. King Xerxes reversed the law that would have killed her people. The bold stance Esther took resolved the situation in favor of the Jews.

Being bold in who we are is not the same as speaking our minds. To be bold is to be brave in uncertain times. It is defined as fearless before danger. It is not arguing when I feel wronged or speaking out on issues when I feel strongly. There is a time and a place to stand for and with others when issues are important. To be bold is to face danger head on to create change for the greater good. We can stand bold and have grace at the same time. Esther did. We can be obedient to the law and to the government without compromising our godly values. Esther did. And we can back ourselves in prayer and choose our actions wisely so that our voices will speak. Esther did that, too.

For many years, women have taken a bold stance for what they believe. Many of the things we enjoy today are a result of a woman boldly asking for the right to do so. Without brave women, we might not have equality as we do now. We might not have college degrees or own houses. There is a lesson on dedication and standing boldly in each of their stories, just as there is in Esther's life. Each woman's story is a tale of a time when grace and class had to intersect with the desire to make a difference.

Women like Marie Curie pursued science with a passion despite their male critics. Or Florence Nightingale, who insisted against her father's will to take care of injured soldiers. Rosa Parks sat for her beliefs amid a hot social climate, and Amelia Earhart encouraged women to pursue their goals as a challenge. These women stood for the passionate pursuit of their craft in the face of gender inequality. The quality of life for a woman has increased drastically because of the bold stances these women took. We are afforded rights and privileges, working in careers and positions beyond what many of them thought possible.

Scripture tells us, "Therefore, since we have such hope, we are very bold" (2 Cor. 3:12). It is through our hope in Christ we can make our bold declarations. It is here in the grace of God we find the balance necessary to state our message with confidence.

In other places, the Bible cautions us about standing boldly. In Proverbs 21:29 we read, "The wicked put up a bold front, but the upright give thought to their ways." To speak out with our words and actions without thinking through them is a bold front. It looks a lot like bravery. It looks and feels scary, as if danger were present. But lashing out without thinking or on terms that are for personal gain is only a front. It is pretending. It is an attempt to gain recognition and not genuinely standing for what is right or good for its own sake. On the other hand, the upright or God-fearing will give thought to their choices and actions. They contemplate what they will do and how they will do it. They work in a way that is productive.

In the book of Acts, people began to take note of Peter and John because they confidently spoke about Jesus. Acts 4:13 highlights a moment when the people around Peter and John realized the cause of their declarations. These two men were "unschooled, ordinary men" who had simply spent time with Jesus. They had to boldly declare their belief after the crowds had witnessed Christ's death. And because of their talk and action in the face of fear, people began to believe in their words and gather as the church. Paul and other writers of the New Testament ask specifically for prayers of boldness and confidence so that others will see what God had done.

The bold declarations of Peter and John had a significant impact on the people around them, not because of their nobility or training but because of their dedication to Jesus. It was their confident manner and unshakable faith that gained attention. As a result, many people came to know Jesus and to be baptized into the Spirit. All because of the apostles' confidence and boldness to declare the truth appropriately.

I Am Bold

God often calls on us to stand confidently against the world on matters of our faith. We must stand like a lion, boldly declaring our beliefs without hesitation. Not by blurting comments on social media. Not by protesting and boycotting non-Christian organizations. We stand for our rights as individuals and as a Church by sharing the truth. We speak words of truth and words of grace without compromising the Bible. We love our neighbors and our enemies without sacrificing our values. We pray for the boldness of Christ and the strength to love in the face of danger. We look for opportunities to show others how God intended life to be lived. And we certainly do not put our righteousness on a pedestal with a "holier than thou" mentality.

Stand firm in your faith. Sometimes the best display of boldness we can have is to act according to our faith. We don't always need to use words to disagree, but instead, we can act in a way that represents our faith. Instead of shouting outside the door of abortion clinics, let us support the pregnancy centers that help women make better decisions for their unborn babies. Instead of yelling profanities at suspected sexual abusers, let's be protective of our own bodies and be educated on self-defense. Let's open our churches and homes to people who look different than we do without judgment.

Being bold is not being loud. It is acting with grace and dignity, obedient to God and law, to benefit the greater good. Being bold with respect is hard. Stand up for your values, but don't speak poorly of others in the process. Choose your words and your actions wisely. Act with dignity, honoring God. Don't stir up arguments or bash other people. And don't speak before thinking how your actions will affect others. Use your social media platforms to encourage others instead of declaring your opposing opinion. Bring positive news to your peers at school or work instead of dwelling on the bad news dangled in front of us. Be the voice of light in the world of darkness.

I encourage you to pray fervently before you act. Every act of boldness and courage requires a time of preparation. Before you make a move, be sure it is one God would approve. Let it be full of his grace. Let everything you do be God-honoring so that others will see God at work in you.

Living a Life Bold

How does it look to live your life bold? It's a life of grace and truth. We stand up for the greater good in truth but handle ourselves with grace and propriety. Here is how you can practice living your life bold:

- **Speak with truth *and* grace.** Tension between truth and grace causes us to lean toward one or the other. Balance your truth and your grace.
- **Think before you speak.** Don't get caught up in the need for a quick reply. Think through your words and actions, being sure they fit your character and values.
- **Ask for bold confidence.** Just like the disciples, ask God to give you bold confidence to stand for him.
- **Pray and act.** Always seek God in prayer before you take a stand.

Discussion Questions

1. Who is the boldest woman you know (or know of), and why do you think so?
2. Where do you put up a bold front? And where do you give thought to your ways?
3. Are you bold for Jesus? How?
4. What part of Esther's story do you think is the boldest? Why? Would you have the courage to be as bold as Esther?

NOTES

[1]Weiyi Cai and Scott Clement, "What Americans Think about Feminism Today," New Wave Feminism, *Washington Post*, January 27, 2016, https://www.washingtonpost.com/graphics/national/feminism-project/poll.

[2]Katherine Switzer, "The Real Story," *Katherine Switzer Marathon Woman*, https://kathrineswitzer.com/1967-boston-marathon-the-real-story/.

Thoughts and Reflections

Popular

Popular (adj.): of or relating to the general public; suitable to the majority; frequently encountered or widely accepted; commonly liked or approved.

I made the cheerleading team. I was a sophomore in high school, and I was most certainly a nerd. I was not part of the smart crowd, I had no skill for sports, and I was definitely not one of the pretty girls. No, I was the one shoved in a locker during class changes. I was kicked, tripped, and messed with more times in middle school than I can count. I was part of the marching band, and I was the president of the Future Homemakers of America club. In other words, I was a nobody. Making the cheerleading team came as a complete shock, and it felt like my ticket to popularity.

Except it wasn't.

Sure, I made the team. I practiced like them. I dressed like them. I even began to talk like them. But I never really became one of "them." When practices finished, or games ended, I went back home to the quiet isolation. I watched as the girls had sleepovers, went on dates with boys, and earned the respect of teachers and coaches. I wanted desperately to fit in with the team, or any other group of people. But in the end, I was just as lonely on the team as I was before.

I was still me. Just me.

I wanted to be popular. I wanted to have friends in every class and a place to sit in the cafeteria. I wanted sleepovers and birthday party invitations. I wanted friends who included me because they wanted to, not because a teacher made them. I wanted to be liked.

It turns out popularity would never be my thing. I had a small circle of friends who appreciated me and did all the things teenage girls do. My two friends always felt so small. I have never had crowds surrounding me or multiple people vying for my attention. I craved the attention, but for all the wrong reasons.

"Like" and Follow

The fast-paced, clickable world of social media allows us to make connections. We thumb through lists of people, finding everyone we know, once knew, or wish we knew. We search out celebrities, find friends from the past, and connect with people we may or may not know face-to-face. We sometimes accept friend requests from people we have drifted away from and would prefer not to remember, convincing ourselves we are better Christians if we friend everyone who asks. Even if a large following is not the goal, somehow the number or types of connections we make via our media accounts correlates to a sense of self-worth.

As our number of likes goes up, so does our self-confidence. We attribute our number or status of friends to our self-worth. The more people who depend on us, or even notice us, the more valuable we are to the world. It is as if the number of social media friends we have translates to a salary for being known. We build and build our number in hopes of achieving fame and fortune just for being who we are.

The desire to be popular is the wish of having a friend list. A long list of friends is like a golden ticket of friendship. Sometimes the length of our list is the result of our time rather than our social likability. I can search for any of the hundreds of people from my graduating high school class, or the thousands who went to the same college I did. I can search for the parents at my kids' school, find everyone who attends the same church, or find groups of people who share a common interest. I can send out friend request after friend request, but are they really friends? If you scrolled through your feed right now, how many tweets would you read beginning to end? How many posts would you like? How many comments would you leave?

When my children were young, we found a lot of entertainment in search-and-find books. We could sit and search through a picture of a messy bedroom, looking for the two matching socks or the hidden cake doodled in the amusement park drawing. Or we would look through the hundreds of people to find Waldo, Wendy, and the Wizard in their red and white outfits. It's entertaining and often frustrating! Somewhere in the simplicity of a children's activity, I get aggravated at my lack of skill to see the small pictures in the big picture. When my child would give up and walk away, you would often find me continuing to search and search. I just can't give up until I find all twenty-five things on the list.

I get just as stuck on my social media accounts sometimes. I log in to see what is happening with my friends only to find myself still scrolling several minutes later. If I see a comment from someone I know but I'm not yet connected to, I send a friend request. This leads me to find more people with whom I can connect. It becomes a snowball of clicking and searching for people. We tend to get caught up in searching for more friends and more likability. We thumb through the "people you may know" list and the "mutual friends" box. We add people, trying to fill our five thousand slots.

The next day, when we post that deep, thought-provoking quote from classic literature, it is seen by only ten people. The adorable picture of a baby sitting in the cupboard chomping on Cheerios collects only twelve likes. The baby goat video is watched only three times. The length of our friends list is not adding up to the attention we get. We allow ourselves to get discouraged because people are not responding to our posts and comments. It causes us to wonder about our true likability. We question whether we have real friends.

Pause for a minute and ask yourself this: How many posts on your social media feed do you actually read, and to whom do they belong? How often do you like another's status or photo? Do you even have the brain capacity or time to manage five thousand updates in the average three hours you spend scrolling through social media? Your likability goes beyond your clickability. The digital world says our popularity is determined by how many people click "like" or "follow," that the number on our friend list is proportional to our fame. We become popular or famous by our ability to spread a message to a large audience. Social media creates a fame status that is impressed by our quantity of friendships rather than our quality of content.

Popularity is a lot like fifteen minutes of fame. You can gain fame and popularity quickly in a variety of ways. Perhaps you suddenly became a hero for your part in a local news story. Maybe you created a work of art that gained the attention of many people, or you are selected as teacher of the year in your school district. Or perhaps you make a mean apple pie, gain notoriety for your amazing voice talents, or find yourself with an influx of YouTube views on the crazy stunt video you posted. Your temporary popularity will fade if you cannot produce something to keep it thriving. When you can no longer achieve the results for which you are famous, you are no longer popular.

The use of social media can help extend our fifteen minutes. When we gain this short-lived type of fame, we can quickly add followers and fans to our social media lists. This extends our ability to reproduce results by giving us more exposure. As people begin to follow, they see more of us, and our fame is extended. The more likes and clicks we receive, the more our popularity builds. This cycle continues until we can no longer produce what is drawing in the people.

The constant ability to track people gives us a false sense of having a friendship with those people. Because I can find my favorite band online and learn all about them, I begin to believe I am an invested part of their life. I can spend time investigating my favorite actress, finding out where she was born and all about her childhood. Or I can dig into another person's public social media accounts to find out about Sara's sister Jenny's boyfriend's brother's girlfriend's super cute cousin. Hours of lurking in social media can lead us to a false sense of friendship with those we don't know in person, and the same is true for the one receiving the attention. When all eyes are on me and my popularity, I begin to believe I have a slew of people who know me. My five thousand followers not only know me, but they also like me and will care for me when I need it. The more people who watch me, the more support I have available.

But more eyes does not mean more friendships. Friendships develop in the details. It's getting to know a person and not just snapshots posted on the Internet. Friendship is knowing someone; popularity is driven by the number of people who see me. To see me takes a little time and data, but to know me takes a commitment. Investing in another person's life takes time and conversation.

With a mild effort, you can reduce your conversations to the tweet length of 140 characters or the snap of one simple image. This tactic captures your audience in the fifteen seconds an average person spends on any one particular social media post. Try to reduce your personality, emotions, laughter, and tone to that same 140 character limit, and it's a bit more challenging. How often do you have a conversation with a real friend that lasts only fifteen seconds? Maybe it sounds something like this:

"Hey. Bad day. Jimmy did it. Mom's made dinner. Gotta go."

"Did you see that show? I can't believe it! Let's watch again next week."

"Wanna grab pizza Friday? Bring skates, too. Meeting starting. Got to go!"

Fifteen seconds or 140 characters leaves no time for quality.

Popularity is gained in the quick wit and high-interest of social media posts. It's the eight-second videos or the eye-capturing images. Fame is the quick capture of attention and the ability to continue delivering people the outcome they want.

To be looked upon as trendsetting or even idolized by others is thought to be good. We gain self-satisfaction with every follower. But reaching for fame and fortune can be detrimental. If we are always seeking more likes or more followers, we will leave many people behind. If our focus is on gaining popularity, what is it we are feeding to our current fans? If we are always looking for more, we are not looking at nurturing what we have. A quest for fame can turn into a lonely adventure. We make sacrifices for popularity that leave us with no committed relationships.

We celebrate a milestone of likes but have no one to call to celebrate. The world of gain has isolated us into a space for one. Our selfish collection of more, more, more leaves us with no depth of friendship. We may reach five thousand on-screen, but in real life we feel as if we have nothing.

People ooh and aah over the number of followers or views. The more people who see your stuff, the more people will buy it. If you are a household name, you can convince the world to do cartwheels in a mud puddle in the name of funny videos. Numbers persuade us that we are valued. Somewhere along the way, we become convinced that more followers add up to being a better person. The number of followers and surface-level relationships is a sign of availability and performance. It's a measure of how well we can show our talents and skills. Popularity is a platform. The measure of who you are is what you do from that platform.

More Than Celebrity: Popular by Leadership

Think about the days of Jesus. Though we don't know the details of his childhood, we suspect it was typical of his time. Raised by his mother and earthly father alongside his brothers and sisters, we know that Jesus had no public ministry—no miracles, no teaching, no unique skill set for a child. To everyone around him, he was Mary and Joseph's son, James's brother, or the kid down the block. He'd met a few synagogue leaders and other people nearby, but he was not known as Jesus the Messiah. He was just Jesus, the boy from Nazareth.

Fast forward thirty years or so. Jesus had grown to be a man, just as the other boys his age had grown. No notoriety, no fame, and no popularity. Early in his ministry, he is kicked to the curb by his hometown folks. To them, he was just a boy from a carpenter's family, so when he began to teach and preach in the synagogue, he was not accepted. So much so that the people of his childhood wanted to throw him over the cliff (Luke 4:29). But Jesus did what many refuse to do: he just walked through the crowd and straight out of town.

Jesus did not have instant or sudden popularity. He was often mocked and scorned throughout his earthly ministry. Even so, he continued to do what he was sent to do. He continued to live as God the Father instructed. He followed the laws and kept the commandments. He taught crowds and discipled individuals. He healed the sick. Cared for the lonely. And preached the message of hope and life throughout the land. He did not seek popularity; he sought to lead the people.

In his three years of ministry, Jesus gained many, many fans and followers. When he began healing and casting out demons, the people of the lands near and far tried to get near him. Crowds gathered to hear him speak. Hillsides of people flocked to be near and to be healed. The Bible gives us an abundance of examples of people acting in desperation just to get near him. Like the time four friends opened the panels of the roof to drop their friend next to Jesus in the middle of a very crowded room. Or the time when the woman called out louder and louder, so much that the disciples asked Jesus to quiet her.

Notice how Jesus handled the crowds and the miracles: in quiet. After many of the healings recorded in the Bible, Jesus asks the person healed and those nearby to remain quiet. He often tells them to see to it that no one knows about the healing. He did not want to be a public spectacle or achieve his fifteen minutes of fame. Miracles were not a tool he used to gain popularity, but a method of winning hearts and minds for the Kingdom. After nearly all the large crowd teachings recorded, Jesus's next move is to go away on his own and pray. He frequently needed to pull himself away from the attention. He didn't do teaching or healing so that he would be praised. He carefully selected and performed the miracles he did to show the love and power of the Father to the people who needed to turn their hearts and minds to his work.

Jesus did not seek to be popular, but to be a loving leader. He invested time and energy into people. Though he had many eyes on him, he made time for relationships. Crowds and followers were not his focus. He didn't keep a list of people who liked him or count heads at each event to see if he had more than last time. He cared about shepherding his people and building relationships. He chose to disciple others in everyday life, not just profess from his platform.

In the Gospel accounts, we see this to be true again and again. Think of the time when a woman reaches to touch the hem of Jesus's garment as he walked down the road. Jesus's popularity is recognized here by the crowds following him. Luke tells us the crowds were crushing him or pressing in on him. The Greek word here is also used to refer to choking or squeezing. In other words, the group around was so large he had little personal space. The simple touch of a woman on the edge of his garment stopped him in his tracks to speak to her.

"Who touched me?" Jesus asked. When they all denied it, Peter said, "Master, the people are crowding and pressing against you" (Luke 8:45). In the crowd of many, Jesus felt the touch of one person in particular. He stopped to find her. He wanted to know her. He made space and time in the middle of the crowd. He looked over all the people in attendance who came to "like" and follow him to find the one who sought him as Lord. It was not the large crowd that captured his attention, but the one person who bravely pushed through the crowd to seek him in faith.

I Am Popular

Too often we take a look at our world from a self-built platform. We stand at our own podium and look out over the crowds. We judge our value and our effectiveness by how many people have come to our stadium tour. Our ability to influence others seems only possible from the stage. We buy into the idea of others wanting to be like us as somehow making us more important. Special. Noteworthy.

Instead of looking at how many liked or favorited you on last night's social media post, look at the comments. Have you engaged your friends in a discussion? Is anyone encouraged by your friendship? That's the stuff of likability! Your ability to enlighten and support, to show love in your everyday world, and to live life out loud is worth far more than millions of YouTube views of a commercial selling chips. When we are real and truly engaged in our circle of influence, we are something greater than popular.

Faithful friends are more than a number on a page or the click of a thumbs-up. They are the people who sometimes agree with you and sometimes choose to be okay with your differences. They are not your friend because of your near-celebrity status. Real friends are the people who dive deep into your world to support you in the good and tough times. Instead of spending time searching for a numbered list of acquaintances, spend your time walking along your friend's path with her for a day. Friends spend time investing in each other's lives. Jesus calls this discipleship.

Discipleship is leadership. It's taking someone under your wing and declaring, "I'll be here for you no matter what, reminding you that God is with you always." Discipleship is asking the others about the miracles God has performed that they have kept quiet. It's looking to the Bible together to find out what to do in tough situations. It's praying thanksgiving together. Communing together in remembrance. And creating a relationship of three cords that will outlast every fifteen minutes of fame ever achieved. Leadership by discipleship is what Jesus taught us to do. Not in crowds or from platforms, but among friends.

This world thrives on relationships. God created us to have friends and to be a friend. It's no secret that women thrive on friendships. Even the most introverted girls find comfort in a close friend. Our inner circle of friendship, no matter the size, gives us a space to be a community of females. Girl talk is one of the keys to a woman's relationship with her friends. We need an outlet to express ourselves in words, and to have a conversation with a friend is a God-given gift. If you sort through your own words, chances are most of your words go to one of your two closest friends. It is even more likely that your closest few friends have heard all about your day before you post it on social media.

If our inner circle of devoted friends is so small, why do we strive to increase our number of followers? We let popularity trap us into another game of more is better. The world says the more you get, the better a person you are, so we try to tally as many people as we can into our circle of influence. Instead of adding more and more to our circle, perhaps we should be tightening our circle more and more within the structure of discipleship. Instead of one thin cord of people strung together, let's weave thread after thread of discipleship through our circle, so that it is tight enough to withstand the demands of the world.

Our small circle of discipleship is our platform. It is the place where we can influence others by walking through this world. It's an environment of understanding, of God's Word, and of community unlike any other. As we connect in discipleship, people will want to bring in their people of influence. One at a time, people will be drawn into the relationships created on the foundations of discipleship. From the gradual adding of people, we may become popular in the way Jesus did. People will be drawn to our teaching, advice, and comfort, not because of our name and fame. They will find us because of our compassion and our love. They will begin to follow our ways because they see how we react in a godly manner. Those with whom we are popular will like us because we are pouring out the love of Jesus.

Popularity, as God intended, is not fame or fortune. It's for influence and relationship. When we are known for our continual faithfulness, our compassionate love, and our balance of grace and truth, we are living a life of influence. We are popular because we are a living example of God's intentions. People like Billy Graham, Mother Teresa, and Pope Francis are known as influencers for God. They gained popularity and fame because of the examples they set of God's great love. Vice President Mike Pence and football star Tim Tebow have a popularity that allows them a platform to be influencers for Christ in a way that is unwavering despite the negative feedback of our society. Though their popularity came first, they have found ways to be kingdom influencers from their positions in the spotlight.

Many of us will never reach celebrity status, yet we have the ability to be influencers from our own platforms. Our choices and actions serve as examples that influence our families. Our coworkers will see our example as well. Even the people who shop at grocery stores with us see our examples. Each of these seemingly small platforms can become a place where your personal popularity is a light of godly influence.

The desire to be popular is not inherently negative. We are wired to be influencers, to have relationships that draw in more people. We are not meant to be idols, to be watched and nearly worshipped for what we do. Instead, be popular for the way you treat others. Be known for the way you speak and act. Look after your circle of influence with compassion and togetherness, and take time to get to know people and help them see who is influencing you. And if you find yourself on a platform in the midst of a crowd pushing in on you, be sure to stop to help the people who need to see Christ in you. Being popular is a matter of living the gospel more than fame. When we use our popularity to spread the message of the gospel, our world will be changed.

My high school problem? I wanted to be who *they* liked. I tried to be someone other than me to be liked. I had a few amazing friends in high school who liked me for me. We were not popular or welcomed in every social scene, but we traveled the awkward roads together. My friends didn't look to how many events we went to or how many people we could gather together. They wanted to invest in my life, and I invested in theirs.

Instead of seeking to gain attention and live in an extended fifteen minutes of fame, live your life as a disciple who makes disciples. Invest in helping others grow from the ground up instead of aiming to convince a large crowd to do it your way. God intended relationships to be small and secure. Influencing three people with God's love and power will bring more glory to God than shouting his name from the rooftops in a distracted city.

How will you use your platform? Will you grow it in the spirit of likes and follows, or will you dive deep into the relationships God has planted?

Living a Life of Popularity

How does it look to live a life of leadership? It's a life of influence. Using your platform, make disciples who invest in the lives of others. Here is how you can practice living a life of leadership:

- **Invest in others.** Do things to let others know you care. Get involved in their life, listen to them, and involve them in discipleship.
- **Create a platform.** Live your life in such a way that others come to you for godly wisdom.
- **Forget fame.** Don't try to find your fifteen minutes of fame. It's not about how many people see you, it's about the One who is seen through you.

Discussion Questions

1. Have you experienced "fifteen minutes of fame"?
2. What social media app do you use the most? What is it about that app that draws you in?
3. Think about your last phone conversation. Now, reduce it to just fifteen seconds.
4. Talk about your best friend. How long have you been friends, and how did you meet?
5. When Jesus felt the woman touch the edge of his robe, he stopped. Tell about a time someone stopped what he or she was doing to invest in your life. How did it make you feel? Have you stopped for someone else?

Thoughts and Reflections

6

Available

Available (adj): present or ready for immediate use; accessible, obtainable.

To celebrate our anniversary, my husband and I decided to spend a weekend in the woods, hiking and camping. We planned to load up our tent and gear and head to Hocking Hills, a beautiful state park in southeast Ohio known for its breathtaking hiking trails. We reserved a primitive campsite in the middle of the woods for two nights. We looked forward to being away from the busy season that had become our everyday family life.

The weekend arrived, and we loaded our gear, dropped off our young ones, and headed out. When we arrived, we unexpectedly had to haul our gear several hundred yards from the parking lot to the campsite. It was a hassle to load and unload. We had not physically prepared to be so far off the beaten path, but the extra effort paid off because we had a reward waiting for us. Our site proved to be a serene, quiet spot to rest each night after a full day of hiking the many miles of trails.

The goal of our trip was to unplug and soak in the beauty of nature. What I failed to anticipate was the lack of connectivity. Our aptly named primitive campsite disconnected us from more than just the parking lot: we were completely out of cell phone range. Even though I had planned to turn my phone off, the lack of service for emergencies raised my anxiety. With two young children back home, I held on desperately to the need to be reachable. The idea that I could not be found if something were to happen to one of my children caused panic in my mind.

In real life, my children were more than three hours away in the more-than-capable hands of their grandparents. Any emergency or other need they had would be handled appropriately, and I would be found if necessary. There was nothing I could do from the park to help them at home, and nothing they could do if I were to have an emergency. Yet the fear of the unknown dominated my mind. Because I was not connected and available at all times, I could not relax. I let my unavailability cloud my time of rest and refreshment.

The saving grace of my sanity was our truck's satellite-connected phone that allowed me to check in with home at the end of each day. It was just enough to settle my anxious thoughts and disconnect the next day. Then, and only then, could I take a deep breath and enjoy the world surrounding me.

Some days I want to unplug entirely, but our world is dominated by the immediate. Full disconnection at the speed of life today is an open invitation to anxiety and fear. We rely on our instant access to know what is important. Everything seems to happen at the speed of cell phones. I feel as if I must always be attached to my device. I must be available.

Text Me

Life is instant. In seconds we can get updates from around the world. We video chat, text, and connect on social media at the touch of a button. Our phones are no longer just for calls but join us to one another in a variety of ways. Because they feel like a source of life, we have developed an attachment to our devices that is replacing our human connection.

Technology has evolved since God uttered the words "Let there be . . ." in Genesis 1. He put into motion everything we see and know today. One step at a time our world has changed and molded to what it is now, including the development of modern technology. The Internet and wireless communications are part of a quickly growing system, but they have roots planted in the past.

Modern advances in technology, like the Internet, have been a work in progress since the mid-twentieth century. In the 1960s, the United States Department of Defense used a single network of connecting cables to share information across multiple computers. In the 1970s, scientists designed a TCP/IP system of organization, setting a communication structure to how information passes from network to network within a system of connected computers. It wasn't until the 1990s that the World

Wide Web launched, linking information to people at the click of a computer mouse.[1]

The history of the cellular phone follows a similar progression. World War I caused a significant boom in technology, including the first field phone allowing soldiers to communicate with the base. Several years later, in 1973, an engineer for Motorola made the very first public cellular phone call while walking down the streets. Martin Cooper used his team's brand-new device to call Joel Engel, an engineer at his rival Bell Systems.[2] Cooper's prototype made its way to the business market ten years later in 1983, costing $3,995. In 1989, the first personal use cell phone hit the market—a flip phone with a retractable antenna, resembling a science-fiction-looking communication device you might have seen on TV. In 2002, a device was launched that afforded users a QWERTY keyboard, access to email, and a few handheld games. But many economy and technology experts agree the most significant boost in cell phone technology came in 2007 when Apple launched the iPhone. Apple's guru and CEO Steve Jobs marketed his company's newest device as a phone and personal computer in the palm of the hand.[3]

Texting emerged in the stream of technology, too. The first Short Message Service, or SMS, received on a cell phone arrived in 1992. It simply read, "Merry Christmas." Just a year later, in 1993, the first cell-to-cell message was sent. Thus was born the text message. Messaging systems within social programs and apps have adapted the use of SMS technology (think AOL Instant Messenger and

Facebook Messenger). A steady increase in messaging services has emerged since those early transmissions.

The combining technologies of the Internet, cell phones, and text messaging lends favor to the demand for instant access. Technology usage has snowballed in the recent past. In a 2016 study by the Pew Research Center, 95 percent of Americans over age eighteen owned a cell phone, and 77 percent owned a smartphone.[4] More than 73 percent of America's teenagers also own a smartphone, giving nearly all Americans older than sixteen instant access wherever they may go.

Text-based communication has become a preferred method of contact for multiple reasons. First, a message that is typed (by SMS, email, or other messaging service) is more comfortable than a phone conversation. It allows the sender to think through and process what is said, rather than blurting it out. Second, a phone call or face-to-face interaction is believed to cause interruption to someone else's day, but a text-based message can be opened at the receiver's convenience. And third, text messages are thought to require less immediacy than a phone call. If the sender can wait for an answer, they prefer to text than seek an immediate reply via phone call. Because of this, the phone app itself is no longer earning the top app spot on a smart device.

Beyond phone and text, Americans have instant access to a multitude of services on our smartphones. With one touch of an icon on our home screen, we are connected to digital news, weather, retail outlets, music, video, and social media. Connections across many platforms occur within seconds. We can shop and have items delivered the same day, we can connect live to our friends living in another state, and we can read the news out of Washington within seconds of its occurrence.

How we use technology from the palm of our hand can be examined by looking at the most-used applications, or apps. In 2017, the top-ten most-used apps included the music service Pandora, Google Maps, Google's search engine, and the digital distribution service known as Google Play. The remaining six on the top-ten list are apps that connect us to other people, including Gmail, Snapchat, Instagram, YouTube, Facebook, and Facebook Messenger. Facebook, Facebook Messenger, and Gmail also top the list of apps appearing on user home screens.[5] The connection to others within these social apps gives us access to each other more now than ever before. We can be in contact with someone nearly any hour of any day from any location. The average text message is read within three minutes and will gain response in just ninety seconds.[6] With nearly twenty-two billion texts sent worldwide in a single day, texting is happening continuously at all hours. We are a society of instant access.

With all this access, we have begun to see a demand to be more available than used to be expected in previous generations. Never have people been as attached to their mobile devices as in our current culture. We hardly change rooms without our phones in tow, and many of us will sacrifice promptness if we need to turn back to get a device we forgot. Do you get an actual call from someone because you didn't answer their text within five minutes?

Or get a text from a coworker within seconds of an email arriving in your inbox? Ever get a guilt trip for not answering a call? Because we are dependent on availability, we have a tough time unplugging. And it causes more strife in relationships than we care to admit.

One of the realities we must consider is our view of urgency. For many, the sense of urgency looks more like an emergency. Our need for a rapid response is treated as an emergency. Our anxiety-burdened world has taught us that if our loved ones are not immediately available, they are involved in an emergency. Worry and panic begin to drive our emotions. All of a sudden, our urgency has become an emergency in our minds. We send a text message thinking we don't want to interrupt the receiver, but our environment tells us we should be significant enough to get a reply right away. The longer we wait for a reply, the more urgently we inflate our need for a response. The cycle sends our emotions to overload, and we begin to devalue our relationship, thinking, "Maybe I'm just not important to her." On the receiving end, we tend to get caught in the same cycle. We have welcomed the urgency and emergency of incoming messages. A waiting message burns a hole in our proverbial pocket. We become like Pavlov's dog, answering to the chimes of our phone. It dings, and we get sucked in, unable to focus until we have read or heard the message. It is an interruption that has become accepted and even expected.

The sending and receiving game drives the constant need to have our device with us everywhere. From schools to stores, restaurants, and even church, we almost always know where to reach to find our technology. Beyond carrying our devices wherever we go, many of us take our phones to bed with us. More than 70 percent of parents, 82 percent of teens, and 72 percent of preteens keep their phone within reach of their bed when they sleep.[7] This invites us to be available for extended hours and creates in us a temptation to reach for access first thing when we wake. The dinner table is another place our phones are causing a change in dynamics. Nearly 45 percent of parents and 27 percent of teens and preteens will take calls or texts during family meals. A quarter of all parents agree this is a significant disruption but allow it to happen because of the need to be available.

Disconnecting

Experts in mental health suggest loneliness is on the rise. How can we be lonely with the instant connections and social media threads available at our fingertips? When we are expected to be available to everyone at a moment's notice, we begin to lose sight of who we are to ourselves, leading to a feeling of loneliness. We spend time browsing through the latest updates of our friends, family, and celebrities. For nearly one in five of us women, this task leads to a feeling of loneliness or jealousy of someone else's life. Almost a quarter of us feel like we are missing out, and more than half of us report being bored after a browsing session.[8] We flood our minds with what is happening in the lives of those around us, only to end up feeling personally disconnected from our own.

The feeling of missing out or being disconnected drives us to be more available. We want to continue checking social media and texting our friends to keep up with the world. And the more we strive to be involved, the more we disconnect from the people and places in our presence. When we allow ourselves to be available at the touch of a finger or the sound of a notification, we deprive ourselves of being fully involved in the here and now. If my phone is sitting on the dinner table, I am more likely to check in on my friend than I am the people sitting at the table with me. If I am checking my social media first thing in the morning, I am distracting myself from the quiet that will set the tone for my busy day ahead.

We must create space in our world. This space is generated by disconnecting. We need to make ourselves unavailable to the digital world and fully available to the things God has put in our physical world. We need to turn off our phones or leave them in the other room and have a full conversation with our spouse. We need to put our devices away and be fully present in the lives of our coworkers who are in desperate need of human connection. We need to pause our technology to immerse fully in seeking what God has for us.

We also need to extend the same grace to those with whom we communicate. Our urgency is not always an emergency. Accept a delay in response as okay. Yes, even with our teenagers. Do not allow panic when we are unable to connect, but instead rely on the prayers and petitions to our God who does have instant access at all times.

I'll Get Back to You: Available to Rest

If there is any one person in the Bible who can relate to the concept of continuously available, it is Jesus. Time after time, the Gospels tell us about crowds gathering and people seeking him out. We find rulers and widows and all classes of people asking him to help. And he took his twelve disciples with him nearly everywhere, always teaching them beyond his public words. He rarely had time to be unavailable.

In fact, the Gospel account of Mark provides for us an insight into the available life Jesus lived. The first chapter tells of early mornings to evenings, moving from one healing to another, from location to location, in homes and out in the streets. Very early in the morning, he went to a solitary place to pray, but even then, his disciples came looking for him (Mark 1:35–36). He often told those he healed to keep it quiet, but their excitement poured out of them so much that soon everyone heard and sought after Jesus. Crowds grew. Healings and miracles happened. People came from all around to find him. Jesus became so available to the people that he could rarely enter a town without crowds. He began to take extended stays in more isolated areas outside of the towns and villages. Even then people would come to find him because of the things they had heard of him. He had to be available to the people constantly.

The times when Jesus would exit the scene to rest or to pray, he would seek isolation. He left unannounced to find solitude, a place where he could be alone and unavailable to the crowds—and even to the disciples at times. Mark's

Gospel uses the word *eremos*, which is sometimes translated wilderness or desolate. It is descriptive of a physical place, referring to its uninhabited or lonely state. Jesus chose solitude when he wanted to pray. He withdrew from the crowds, finding isolation that cleared his path for an encounter with the Father. He made himself unavailable to the people in order to focus on God.

In all four Gospel accounts, Jesus sought solitude. He quietly and respectfully made time and space to pray and to rest in the presence of the Father only. In the Gospel of Matthew, Jesus instructs us to do similar when he says, "When you pray, go into your room, close the door . . ." (Matt. 6:6). He desires for us to be alone with him for prayer and rest. He wants us to choose solitude as a way of growing as his disciple.

Mark records for us a time when the disciples grew very weary because so many people demanded their attention. Jesus said to them, "Come with me by yourselves to a quiet place and get some rest" (Mark 6:31). He pulled them away with the intention of rest and isolation. Even then it was not easy, though. Mark continues, telling us that even when Jesus and the disciples left by boat, the crowd followed. For Jesus and the disciples, solitude took effort. It had to be intentional. The same is true for each of us.

Jesus does not expect us to be on call to others all the time. He chose solitude, and he wants us to do the same. In times of solitude and isolation, we can fully focus on God. We can find rest and refreshment, gain wisdom and understanding, and differentiate the world from the Word. In our time alone, we find strength for what is happening around us. We forget to worry about the lack of text messages and turn it over in prayer. We lay down our need for social updates and lift up our desires to do what he wants from us. Solitude is a place to learn to rely on God.

He wants us to rely on him for rest and refreshing. He says, "Come to me, all you who are weary and burdened, and I will give you rest" (Matt. 11:28). He was calling for anyone who was struggling to disconnect to find rest with him. By making solitude with him a priority, we find a place to be unavailable to the world while becoming fully available to God. He still calls us to this regular time of rest. Struggling with loneliness? Rest in him. Can't keep up with life? Rest in him. Need to disconnect from the constant demand to be available? Rest in him!

When God had created the universe he, too, rested. Genesis 2:3 says, "Then God blessed the seventh day and made it holy, because on it he rested from all the work of creating that he had done." The Hebrew word *shabath* is used here as rest. Used eighty-eight times in the Old Testament text, God puts into his plan for his people the concept of rest. Rest was defined in creation and throughout the Old Testament, not because a break was necessary but because the relationship was necessary.

The concept of a Sabbath, the Anglicized word for *shabath*, became a tradition or ritual in Jewish worship. Religious practices enforced the Sabbath as a day when no work could be done. In the days of Jesus, we see how this created trouble. Jesus continued to do his work on the Sabbath, like when he and his disciples collected grain in the field as they passed through (Mark 2:23). Both collecting food and walking distances were considered acts of labor and were therefore prohibited among the Jewish people on the Sabbath. Jesus often participated in activities on the Sabbath that caused the religious leaders to dispise him.

The Jewish leaders of Jesus's time upheld the Sabbath as a time God set aside for himself. Many people still do. Jesus knew the truth of the Sabbath: "The Sabbath was made for man, not man for the Sabbath" (Mark 2:27). The purpose of the Sabbath is for the benefit of people. It's intended to be a time set aside for renewal, created so that we will take intentional time for God. The Sabbath is not a day of nothing in order to rest, but a day or time set aside as holy. It is a time set aside to look at what God has done and find what he is doing next. It is prayer and worship. It's spending a day of rest with God the Creator, admiring what he has done. Rest is not a mandate or a stop to everything. It is a purposeful time to be available only to God.

To find solitude and rest is to be unavailable to the desires of the world. It's pressing pause on the texting. It's turning off the social media. It's making yourself temporarily unavailable to others so that you can be available to him.

I Am Available

We do not need to be available at the ring of our phone or the click of a button. Sometimes we need to check out of our technology and check in to the peace we find in his presence.

The last time I left my cell phone at home, I nearly panicked. I was beyond worried something would happen to one of my young boys, and I feared I would not know until it was too late. My husband was at home caring for them, and I had only run up the road for a quick appointment. He certainly could find me if he needed. And what could I have done anyway?

I survived that hour with no instant access. Instead of communicating via my electronic device, I had a full conversation with my preteen daughter. I was not distracted by the updates and messages that frequently chirp for my attention. I didn't scroll through my social media to see what new meals my girlfriends were cooking or what accolades the other kids at school were receiving. Instead, I laughed with my child. We talked about life as a girl. The moment wasn't grand, but it was significant. We unintentionally created space for a relationship.

After that day, I started thinking about how much time I spent focused on my technology. Waiting in line, downtime at home, and even car rides had become a time to pick up my device. I was attached to the convenience, afraid that if I didn't sneak a glance I would miss something in the world. But what was I missing in my own world when I fixed my eyes on the screen? I was staring at the things I didn't have instead of the beauty around me. I watched what other moms were doing with their kids instead of what my own children were doing next to me. I have tried to put down my gadgets more often since then, but it's not always easy.

It's not easy to disconnect. It is difficult to leave technology behind when, without its instant access, we imagine worst-case scenarios in our minds. But it's important to put our gadgets aside and make room in our lives for ourselves, our families, and our relationships with God. Being unavailable is important to our family and our self. If we are attached to our devices, we cannot look up to see the beauty God has created in our world.

Disconnect with technology and reconnect to your relationships. Assure yourself and others that if there is a true emergency, you will be found. And begin to set boundaries that free you from the need to be always available. Find solitude with Christ.

Living a Life of Availability

How does it look to live a life with rest? We must make time and space for being available only to God. Here is how you can practice living a life of rest:

- **Set limits.** Limit your time with technology. Set boundaries for where you will and will not take your device. Turn your technology off when you do not want to be interrupted.
- **Be intentional.** Let your friends and family know of your plans. Ask them to honor your time by not interrupting.
- **Practice prayer.** Do as Jesus instructed and go to a special place to pray where you will not be distracted, and do not take any devices with you.

- **Begin your day well.** Instead of going straight to your phone, begin your day with prayer or worship. Read your Bible instead of your texts. Get your day started with joy instead of the demands of people.
- **Observe a Sabbath.** Set aside a time each week to stop and focus on what God has done in your life.
- **Find solitude.** It's okay to be alone. Seek out times to pull away by yourself.

Discussion Questions

1. Tell about a time you were out of cell phone range. How did the disconnect make you feel?
2. When did you receive your first cell phone? Do you have a smartphone now? What app do you spend the most time on during your day?
3. Discuss the pros and cons of having devices at the dinner table.
4. Do you set aside a time and place to pray? If you wanted to, what would it look like in your life?
5. How do you set boundaries regarding your time and availability with your friends and family?
6. Do you observe a weekly Sabbath? Do you do it out of habit, or do you use it to develop relationships? What do you put aside on your Sabbath, and what do you do instead?
7. How can you make solitude a priority in your life? What does solitude look like in your world?

NOTES

[1]Evan Andrews, "Who Invented the Internet?," History Stories, *History*, December 18, 2013, http://www.history.com/news/ask-history/who-invented-the-internet.

[2]"The First Mobile Phone Call Was Placed 40 Years Ago Today," *Fox News*, April 3, 2013, http://www.foxnews.com/tech/2013/04/03/first-mobile-phone-call-was-placed-40-years-ago-today.html.

[3]"The History of the Mobile Phone," The Switch, *Washington Post*, September 9, 2014, https://www.washingtonpost.com/news/the-switch/wp/2014/09/09/the-history-of-the-mobile-phone/?utm_term=.06b6a03c6a13.

[4]"Mobile Fact Sheet," Internet & Technology, *Pew Research Center*, February 5, 2018, http://www.pewinternet.org/fact-sheet/mobile.

[5]Avery Hartmans, "The 10 Most Popular Apps People Keep on Their Home Screens," *Business Insider*, August 26, 2017, http://www.businessinsider.com/most-popular-apps-people-keep-on-their-homescreens-2017-8/#1-facebook-10.

[6]Kenneth Burke, "73 Texting Statistics That Answer All Your Questions," *Text Request*, May 24, 2016, https://www.textrequest.com/blog/texting-statistics-answer-questions.

[7]"6 Tech Habits Changing the American Home," *Barna Research Group*, April 18, 2017, https://www.barna.com/research/6-tech-habits-changing-american-home.

[8]"Women Report Mixed Feelings about Social Media," *Barna Research Group*, August 17, 2016, https://www.barna.com/research/women-report-mixed-feelings-social-media.

Thoughts and Reflections

7

Happy

Happy (adj): enjoying or characterized by well-being and contentment; expressing, reflecting, or suggestive of happiness; glad, pleased; having or marked by an atmosphere of good fellowship.

It was August of 2005. Awake before the sun, I dressed in my team jersey and tied my hair up. I pinned on my race bib, number 617, ready for my first and only sprint triathlon. At the beginning of the race, I was a ball of nerves. I inched my way to the back of the pack. Clueless. I eased my way into the water as nearly the last person to start the race. I swam 750 meters in Lake Norman, biked 20 kilometers in the gentle hills of North Carolina, and then ran 5 more kilometers to the finish line.

The end of the race was marked by flags and banners, an inflatable tunnel, and hundreds of people cheering. A random stranger shouted out, "You've got this 6-1-7!" I made it. My husband, my sister, and a few of our local friends were among the crowd to see me finish. I don't remember my final finish time. I don't remember any of the people I competed against, or any of the training sessions from the months before the race. What I do remember is how good it felt to finish. It was a happy moment.

When I think back to the days of training, I am not sure what compelled me to do such a crazy thing. Yet the end of that race is a memory I will not forget. I accomplished a goal. My friends and family, even random onlookers, supported me to the end of the race. I was not awarded a special prize, and I did not break any records. It didn't lead to a career or drastically change my daily life. In fact, most of what I have from it are the memories made at the finish line.

I have one photo to prove my day: a picture of myself post-race. I have this cheeky smile plastered across my face with my friends and family at my side. I don't remember who snapped it, or even when exactly it was taken, but it is a picture that reminds me of how I felt as I stood at the finish line. I remember the overwhelming emotion of happiness as I took my place next to my crew of cheerleaders. I had taken on a considerable challenge, and I had completed it. It was a moment of genuine happiness.

If I had to record my top-ten happiest moments of life, it would make the list. It will probably be there forever.

A World of Happy-Go-Lucky

Happy is like a song we sing. Bobby McFerrin told us not to worry and be happy in 1988, and in 2013, Pharrell Williams invited us to clap along if we know how happiness felt. Happiness is represented by a smile on our face or a laugh out loud. It is excitement and pleasure and all the good feels wrapped into one simple word. Happy is an adjective used to describe a feeling of good. It's the reaction of a person when something is pleasurable or content. Happiness is evidenced by the smile on someone's face or the twinkle in her eye. It can be heard through laughter and felt through tears. It's a simple feeling we have all experienced at some point in time.

Happy times are typically moments we remember. Moments of celebration. Those times of laughter and pride. Seasons of accomplishment. Graduation ceremonies and parties. Wedding celebrations, baby births and adoptions, extraordinary gifts, and other good times. They fill the spaces of our memories with good things, evoking a fresh feeling of happy every time we remember. Memories of a time when everything seemed to come together for good. We long to live in the constant feeling of happiness.

The happiness of moments as we know them are temporary. The good moments always fade back to a normal pace of everyday life. We trade the highs of celebration for the routine pace of normal. This transition often leaves us feeling unsteady. We crave life in the highs with laughter and celebration, but more often find ourselves in the mundane rhythm of normal life. Happy wanes to tolerable.

When happy begins to fade, we quickly look for more opportunities. We start to search out the next moment we will smile. The next reason to have a good time. We claim that "if only" were to be true, we could and would be happy. Things are sought after. We aspire for better cars, more toys, a bigger house, and other worldly things to experience the feeling of happiness. The same is applied to our situations. A better job or a salary increase will lead me to happiness. Another college degree or a new location will help create my happiness. A new significant other will bring happiness. We search and search for an avenue that will lead us to feel happy.

For some, the first stop on this journey to happiness is money. Often in today's social circles, we will hear the cliché "money can't buy happiness," yet it is the first thing people seem to try. It's money we seek to get so that we can purchase things to make us happy. We frequently look to these material things to make us happy. A woman with a closet full of shoes for every season must feel happy. A sports-loving man with tickets to the sold-out Super Bowl game ought to be happy. A kid eating a sticky rainbow sucker, a teenager receiving his first set of keys, or a woman seeing a sparkling diamond ring in a little black box are experiencing happy moments all bought with the power of money.

Think of lottery winners. The allure of winning thousands, if not millions, of dollars caused the US population to spend $73.5 billion on traditional lottery tickets in 2016.[1] An estimated ninety million people take the chance at winning the jackpot. Most winners regularly bought a ticket week after week until they won. They are average people working regular jobs and living ordinary lives, with many living near the government's threshold of poverty. With a better chance of being struck by lightning than holding the right combination of numbers, most lucky winners are overtly happy with their new earnings. Winners spend their money on elaborate vacations, upgrading their home, purchasing a second home, and high-end cars. Several winners reportedly paid off mortgages and car loans for friends using a portion of their winnings.

If money and happiness are directly connected, lottery winners should be king of the happiness hill. However, the quick win and loss take a toll on the families, and many winners later report they wish they had never played. Seventy percent of lottery winners end up broke after just seven years. From elaborate spending to social pitfalls like drugs and gambling, lottery winners tend to spend their winnings faster than expected.

Extra cash in hand should be a catalyst for happiness if happy is something to be purchased. In February of 2008, President George W. Bush signed the Economic Stimulus Act, issuing tax refunds to millions of Americans in hopes of boosting the economy. The purpose of the act was to put money into the hands of consumers so that they would spend it on products made in the United States. For every dollar sent back to the people, $1.19 purchased goods and services in the remaining year. This spending boom boosted the economy but contributed little to the overall health of the people. The short-term excitement generated by extra spending money faded into memory, making no long-term impact on the happiness of the American people. By no means was the act intended to help the mental health of the United States, but it is evidence of the truth that money to spend and happiness are not directly connected.

Winning the lottery, getting a salary increase, or buying better things seem to be the prizes our culture associates with happiness. The more money we have, or the better our goods, the happier we are supposed to be. We have fallen into the habit of letting material possessions, money, idols, and experiences be our happiness. Advertising professionals use this principle to sell us more stuff. When we see a new item as something better than what we have, we quickly attribute to it a happiness value. If I can receive this item, I will be the equivalent of this much happier. Advertisers and marketing professionals find new angles to make their product appear to give you just what you need, thereby making you happy. It's the phenomenon of awareness.

When we become aware of what we *could* have, we are no longer happy with what we *do* have. Think about infomercials. In an infomercial you hear, "why settle with," or "why fumble with." Most will compare our everyday product's difficulty with their better solutions. It's creating in us a feeling that we could upgrade to something better. The problem with this thinking is that we already have the necessary tools. The advertisers are playing on our awareness. The audience is now aware of what they do not have, but for "just two payments of . . . plus shipping and handling," they too can have it. "Happiness comes at a cost" is the root of the idea that money can buy happiness.

If money is not fulfilling our need for happiness, we turn to relationships. We look for someone who can make us happy. A husband becomes responsible for a wife's happiness in how he treats her or what gifts he gives her. A boyfriend is expected to be giving of his time and effort to make us happy. A best friend is called on to fix our unhappiness. Relationships are expected to be fulfilling and blissful in every aspect of life.

Relationships built solely on the need to make each other happy quickly crumble. When a best friend chooses truth over satisfaction, it is easy to pull away because of hurt feelings. If the relationship is rooted in making the other happy, an action like honesty can cause the relationship to suffer. Truth in love is often lost for the sake of satisfaction. We rely on each other to bring happiness instead of loving the other enough to walk through other emotions together.

Marriages struggle when happiness is the focus. When one partner begins to disappoint the other, we begin to withdraw our efforts. We walk the path to coexistence instead of love. Too often in our society, the struggle to make your partner happy fails, sometimes resulting in infidelity and marital unfaithfulness. Divorce and unfulfilling marriages are happening across the world because of the dependency on relationships for personal happiness.

The third tangible happiness we seek comes in our location. Happiness comes from a vacation or a new adventure. It comes in the form of a weekend getaway or a week of wandering. A trip to the beach or a hike in the mountains. A trek to another country will help me find perspective and happiness. Even a mission trip with the church becomes a place we look to for happiness. The change in latitude is a spark for a change in attitude.

Moreover, our long-term location is flagged as a happiness marker. We begin to look to relocation and a change of lifestyle to fulfill our emotions. If my house were bigger, I could be happy. My neighborhood, my school, my neighbors could all be better. Even my office or my local coffee shop are expected to provide a sense of happiness.

We search for happiness in our job status. The better a job, the more happiness I will have. We convince ourselves a new job or a promotion at our current one will make us happy. A new coworker, a new title, or a new salary will be the source. Sometimes a new career path is our solution. Our employment status and importance within the company provide a reason to be happy.

Happy as an Emotion

I once saw a sign in a high school girls' restroom that read, "Happy girls are the prettiest." The well-meaning message is intended to express that a smile or other joyful expression is what makes a girl beautiful more than any physical feature she may have. It struck me as odd, as if the emotion of happiness is to be continuously expected of every girl. Are we not allowed to have sad days? Can we not get angry or scared? If we base our beauty on our emotions, it will change day to day or moment to moment.

By searching for a worldly reason to be happy, we are continually looking, but never really finding. The moments of happy in life are fleeting—passing by us in quick, pleased moments. The high-speed pace of emotion cannot sustain the feeling of happy over time. When one moment fades, we quickly begin searching for another.

In the process, we forget the moments of happy and the sources of lasting joy that are in our world. Holding on to the things of this world that are supposed to make us happy will rob us of enjoying the things we already have. Happy in the context of social circles requires us to seek more. More money. More relationships. More stuff. More vacations. The constant need for more leads to the rejection of the things we have acquired. A happier relationship results in breaking another. The happiness of more stuff requires you to get rid of things you once enjoyed.

Instead of finding joy, we make attempts to connect happiness with our present circumstances. We begin to believe that getting everything to swing in our favor is the key. This search for things that lead to happiness makes us wish we could sprinkle a few drops of Harry's *Felix Felicis* in our morning coffee. If only we had a little luck, circumstances would go just the right way and then we would be happy. In our minds, we've told ourselves that the only times that we're happy is when things go our way. But sometimes, just as the characters of J. K. Rowling's adventures discover, if you believe that circumstances are in your favor, you may act in new ways that lead to positive results, no luck needed. I can also think of many times that I have found moments of genuine happiness during times that were very difficult and painful. Those moments have become memories of joy that keep me going when life becomes difficult again. Our circumstances do not limit our ability to be joyful, but our search for momentary happiness based on our circumstances does.

The Joy of Mary and Mary: Happy in the Moment

Perhaps a better phrase for the bathroom sign I mentioned, and one I would believe, is "Joy makes you beautiful." We don't have to live in a moment-after-moment state of happiness. Instead, we can take root in the idea of joy as a thread connecting those moments. The memories of happy times can stand out in our mind as reminders, giving us joy for life. The exhibition of joy is beautiful.

The Bible has a lot to say about joy. Used 218 times in the New International Version, joy is a common theme for Christian living. We find kings and prophets, even whole nations, shouting with joy to the Lord. When we look at the Bible's uses for the word joy, we can see its reference to the long-lasting memories evoked rather than the temporary emotional response. Many times, when referring to joy, Scripture recounts blessings and fond memories. Psalm 126:3 says, "The Lord has done great things for us, and we are filled with joy." Memories of such happy moments fill us with joy.

Two verses later, the psalmist writes, "Those who sow with tears will reap with songs of joy" (Ps. 126:5). God knows that tears of sorrow will flow. The emotion of sadness will pass, and from it, we will find joy. Joy will come on the other side because of our faith. It will be the outcome of watching what God does in us and through us during our times of tears. Even the memories of sadness will turn into lasting joy.

Mary Magdalene and "the other Mary" are recorded as having experienced pure joy. Matthew records the two women as the first to visit the tomb of Jesus after the Sabbath had ended. When they arrived, an earthquake and the appearance of an angel evoked in them an emotional response of fear. But the angel appeared and spoke to the women, showing them that Jesus was no longer in the grave. The angel allowed them to see with their own eyes and then sent them to tell the disciples. The Scripture says, "The women hurried away from the tomb, afraid yet filled with joy, and ran to tell his disciples" (Matt. 28:8). The emotion of fear dominated their brain response, but the memories of lasting joy are present in their minds. Despite the fear of their current circumstances, remembering the Jesus who once walked with them brought gladness. They were terrified by what was happening with their beloved, yet satisfied with the memories he had created.

This sense of joy in the midst of other emotions can be felt in the teachings of Jesus, too. When preaching to the crowd during the Sermon on the Mount, Jesus began with a list of blessings. The word Jesus used here is the Greek word *makarios*, which is translated as blessed and as happy. In this well-known teaching, Jesus provides a list of situations in which we are to be blessed or happy. But how are we to feel happy in times of mourning, hunger and thirst, or persecution? What causes us to be happy when we need to be peacemakers?

Jesus is calling us to be happy and joyful in times of uneasiness. Our emotions can cause our reactions to be in fear, to be downcast or poor in spirit, or even to give compassion and mercy to others through peace and gentleness.

These things are connected to our humanness, but our joy is connected to our holiness. Joy is a gift given by God. It is a fruit of the Spirit, delivered to every believer who walks in faith. We can experience every emotion of humankind and not lose our joy.

Joy is not a here and gone thing. And it doesn't overrule other feelings. If we want to find joy, we must remember the moments of happiness. Culture thinks a smile and a laugh should be ever-present, but it's the comfort of knowing what has happened and what will happen that leads to satisfaction. When James penned the words, "Consider it pure joy, my brothers and sisters, whenever you face trials" (James 1:2), I believe he was reminding us that what is happening will soon be a memory. Trials are inevitable. They are frustrating, difficult, and often painful. But when God walks us through to the other side, we are certainly going to experience a moment of happiness. The memory of that happy moment will forever become a part of our joy. The next time you are facing a trial, consider it joy in the making.

The Joy and Happy Connection

According to neuroscientist Antonio Damasio, emotions and feelings are distinct things.[2] Emotions are the physical response to a situation. The increase in heart rate, the widening of the eyes, or the tightening of muscles are the body's responses that science labels as emotion. They are transient, changing according to our environments and situations. Feelings, on the other hand, are the response in our brain to the emotions we have. It's the storage process, or mind mapping, of situations and events.

Given this scientific theory, to set up camp in a constant feeling of happiness would require our environments and situations to always provoke bodily responses of an emotion of happiness. Neurotransmitters in the brain are the signaling device of emotion. Various combinations of different neurotransmitters are released to create the varying emotions. When a moment of happiness occurs, a mixture of brain chemicals is released, giving us the emotional response we call happy. Because the compounds are produced as our body's way of signaling a smile or laugh, they are also short-lived. As the moment of happiness ends, so will the physical response, allowing our bodies the ability to experience a range of emotion rather than always feeling the same thing.

In his 2011 TEDx talk, social science researcher Michael Norton presented to a room full of business-oriented listeners in Cambridge, Massachusetts, that, indeed, money can buy happiness.[3] His research on how we spend money provides evidence that the way we spend our money has a substantial impact on our happiness. Research on the way college students, families, sales teams, and social clubs rated their happiness as a result of spending money on themselves or spending it on someone else was collected and analyzed. By far, the people who spent money of any amount on others had a higher level of happiness at the end of the day. By giving to others, we create a greater, longer-lasting sense of happy. When we choose to give to others, we are developing or expanding a relationship, and it is relationships that science says make a person happy. In fact, relationships and experiences are the most significant factors in the happiness of a person.

Other factors of happiness according to science include slowing down to take in the moment (or "stopping to smell the roses," as some would call it), physical exercise, and mindfulness (or the consciousness of the present moment). What is it about being in the moment or helping others that creates happiness? Being present or being involved in the life of another gives a person a sense of purpose. The human condition reaches for meaning in all aspects of life. When we give to another person—in money, in time, or in an experience—we are creating meaning in the relationship. Both the giver and the receiver get a piece of the happiness, but the giver also perceives a sense of purpose. It is as if she has done something with meaning.

When we talk about lasting happiness, we are looking for joy. Joy is not the evoking of a temporary emotion, but the prolonged feeling of satisfaction. Joy is like remembering the feeling of happy even when the chemicals of it are not being emitted. Somewhere our brains remember what it feels like to smile and laugh, allowing us to pull that memory even when we are not in a happy moment.

Living a Life of Joy

How does it look to live a life of joy? It's a life of remembering. We take in the times of happiness and record them. We pull them up when times get tough or when we need a reminder. Joyful living is remembering who God is and what he has done for you. Here is how you can practice living a life of joy:

- **Reflect.** Take time to remember and thank God for moments.
- **Spend your money.** Give to others generously, because giving creates more happiness than receiving.
- **Be present.** Hang out in the now moments, taking in all the things God has placed around you at every step.
- **Consider it joy.** Look at hardship as the creator of new joy. Remind yourself of the hardships you have been through and the work of God's hand throughout your life.

Discussion Questions

1. Record a list of your ten happiest moments. Discuss an item on your list. Why did it make you happy?
2. Where have you tried to find happiness? Did you find it, and how long did it last?
3. Often discontentment begins with awareness, or finding out what you might be missing. Tell of a time you experienced a discontent feeling because of a sudden awareness.
4. Think about a time you spent money on yourself, and a time when you spent it on someone else. How did each make you feel that day? How did you feel the next day, and the next week? Do you agree that

money can buy happiness when you are spending it on someone other than yourself?

5. Reflect on a few hardships in your life. Are you able to find joy at the end of each journey?

6. How do you follow Paul's instructions to "consider it all joy"?

NOTES

[1]Chris Isidore, "We Spend Billions on Lottery Tickets. Here's Where All That Money Goes," *CNN Money,* August 24, 2017, http://money.cnn.com/2017/08/24/news/economy/lottery-spending/index.html.

[2]Manuela Lenzen, "Feeling Our Emotions," *Scientific American*, accessed March 24, 2018, https://www.scientificamerican.com/article/feeling-our-emotions.

[3]Michael Norton, "How to Buy Happiness," TEDxCambridge, November 2011, https://www.ted.com/talks/michael_norton_how_to_buy_happiness#t-639431.

Thoughts and Reflections

Conclusion

Defining My Identity as a Masterpiece

When I was a little girl, I did what most little girls do—I dreamed of what my life would be like when I grew up. I imagined myself wearing those cute housewife dresses and aprons, baking and cooking homemade meals that were on the table when my husband walked in the door and shouted, "Honey, I'm home!" Our 2.5 kids and our little dog would hug their father, then sit with perfect manners to eat all of the vegetables on their plates. We would smile through the whole meal, clean up together, then sit and watch a television show. Life was going to be like *The Brady Bunch*, and I couldn't wait to grow up and make it come true.

And then I grew up. I posed for all the perfect housewife cameras, believing that if I could fake it long enough,

I would make it. In reality, I had to have a job to make ends meet, so I was often running out the door as my husband walked in. My kids preferred jumping off the couch to sitting on it, eating ice cream instead of veggies, and watching Netflix in their rooms. We went through more drive-throughs and dirty clothes than any family I knew. Cleanup time . . . what's that? In the longest days of life, my world felt more like the never-ending questions and messy challenges of *Double Dare* than the happy, fun-filled days of *The Brady Bunch.*

After my false world crashed in 2011, I learned to embrace the mess a little more. I'm okay with dirty dishes in the sink when guests come over. I schedule time to spend with my tribe so I can feel like I am giving them my full attention, even when other projects are not finished. And I have learned to find the happy moments as they are happening and not through the lens of a camera. I can't say I live a redefined life every single day, but I more easily recognize my thinking when I get caught up in the world's labels.

The world tries to form us to its definitions of beautiful, perfect, and successful. But God says we are beautiful from the start, we are complete when we give him our all, and our successfulness is based on our faith in him more than in our trophy collection. His definitions are different from the ones we find in *Merriam-Webster* or *People* magazine. He is not a God of outdoing others or earning approval. He wants more for us than the pettiness of trying to be good enough for others.

Created to Be Me

God created man in his image and according to his likeness (Gen. 1:26). By creating man in his image, God made man to have a resemblance to him. We are not copies or replications, but instead, we are made to have an alikeness. We have qualities of how we look that are like the way God looks. When the Bible says we are made in his likeness, it is referring to the model or shape we take. It is our physical form. In other words, we are made in the form of God, *and* we resemble his image with our features.

Think about children and parents. A daughter can resemble the look of her mom by having the same eye color or skin tone, but she can also take her shape with her height and stature. Our physical features are reflections of God's form, and our image reflects his details.

The Bible tells us we are created in the image of *Elohim*, the name for the strong creator God. Not the all-powerful or the Great I AM God, but Elohim, the strong creator. This is the same God who made the universe from nothing, who spoke a word and things were made. In his form and fashion, we are created as a unique creation. Different and diverse, but all by the works of the creator.

The detail of our look and our form are intricate creations. We are knit together in our mother's womb, where he chooses every aspect of our appearance and character (Ps. 139:13). He is not a factory God who pulls the handle and molds each baby into the same form. Every person is handcrafted. You are put together in the form and fashion of God by the hand of God.

As we grow physically and spiritually, we are molded more and more into his image. We become reflections of his character. The more we let our lives be molded by his power, the more we reflect this true definition of who we are with authenticity. It is when we do not hide who we are that we reflect his glory more than our own: "[W]ith unveiled faces [we all] contemplate the Lord's glory [and] are being transformed into his image with ever-increasing glory" (2 Cor. 3:18).

To be the image and likeness of God is to embrace our physical self. Love who you are just because you are made that way. Every detail of you is perfectly designed. Care for yourself for the same reason. Act, dress, and live in a way that shows your likeness. You and I and every person on the earth bear the lineage of God. We cannot deny our Father because we are made in his image. We are not replicas, but we are reflections. We must reflect the qualities God gave us and not seek the merits of the sinful world. He made us beautiful and complete. He calls us to be appropriate and wise, to speak for the good of the whole, and to be disciples. He wants us to find joy and rest as we go through life. This is the image he wants for us. These are the labels he wants us to wear.

Genesis 2 tells us woman was made to be a helper, just as the Holy Spirit is to be a helper or aide. Woman is made to help bear the image of God. He calls us to be helpers, not dividers. We do not need to be worldly equals to have importance and significance because we are not the same. We each have a role to bear the same image differently, as one who comes alongside and supports, who reminds others of the image we carry. When we can live life in the image of God, fitting into the labels he chose and not concerning ourselves with the world's expectations, we will live as the masterpieces he designed.

God's Masterpiece

A masterpiece is an exceptional piece of an artist's work. It is his pride and joy, the thing by which he is most enthralled. Leonardo da Vinci's *Mona Lisa* and Vincent van Gogh's *Starry Night* are incredible works of art that have long outlasted the artists themselves. The storytelling of Jane Austin and Toni Morrison, the music of Bach and Beethoven, the film works of George Lucas, and the stage presence of Fred and Ginger linger as the best among their fields. The beauty and artistry of many masterpieces are still shared today.

But a masterpiece is not created at the first touch of a brush or a single press of a key. It takes time and effort, refining and defining. It takes courage to start and concentration to finish. Every artist has a masterpiece, whether famous or not. Painters, potters, writers, filmmakers, and musicians alike have something they have worked again and again until they were satisfied with its greatness.

Paul calls man God's masterpiece in his letter to the church in Ephesus (Eph. 2:10). The Greek word *poiema*, translated in the New International Version as workmanship, refers to the handcrafted nature of man. God created us in his likeness and has worked us, formed us, and refined us into his best. His masterpiece.

We are like created works of art: precious and beautiful. We become masterpieces by the works of his hand. He molds us and makes us into godly women by defining us according to his labels, not the labels of the world. He desires for us to leave behind what is necessary for worldly success. The best creations in the world are nothing compared to the works of God. It is when we give up the desire to be the world's stunning art that we become the masterpiece of the God who defines all creation.

Find rest and relationship as God's beloved creation, reflecting who he is with everything you are inside and out. Let him mold you and make you into the things he loves about you. Let him form you and shape you into his daughter. Lay aside what others want you to be. What others may see for you is restricted to the world's lower-level view of the story. Instead, be God's masterpiece: the gloriously created work of his greater story.

Identity in Christ

If we want an example of a woman who lived authentically according to her identity in Christ, seeking glory for God and not worrying about the thoughts of others, we can find one in Mary, the sister of Lazarus. In John 12, we find Mary doing what she thinks is worthy of Jesus without caring what the others in the room thought of it.

Six days before Passover, at a dinner given to honor Jesus, we find Martha serving and Lazarus sitting at table with Jesus. This is likely the first time Jesus has returned to Bethany since raising Lazarus from the dead, and many had gathered to celebrate. Mary loved Jesus and wanted to honor him in all she did. So, after dinner, she let down her hair and brought out her jar of expensive oil. She poured her pure, fragrant oils over Jesus's feet and used her hair to wipe them clean.

The others in the room must have looked at her sideways. Oils like this were used in lavish funerals to prepare a body for death. Sometimes left as a family heirloom, the jar Mary used here would have been valued at more than a year's pay for the average worker. Beyond the expense, a woman letting her hair down in public was considered disrespectful, the washing of feet was a job for the servants, and the idea of preparing someone for burial while he was still alive seemed ridiculous. Mary's actions did not fit with what people thought she should do.

When Judas confronted Jesus about her actions, Jesus defended her on account of her devotion. "Leave her alone. . . . It was intended that she should save this perfume for the day of my burial" (John 12:7). Jesus recognized her intentions, even if she did not yet know it. Her actions were perceived by Jesus as honoring, while Judas thought of them as wasteful.

I love how Mary acts in obedience to her desire to honor Jesus. She isn't worried about Judas; she doesn't concern herself with the cost of the oils, hoping her choice of perfumes is extravagant enough to make her look rich. She simply and humbly acts to exalt Jesus by doing what she could with what she had. Living authentically is doing what we can to honor God. It is using our life to give him the glory no matter how we look to the world. God has continued to lavish his gift of love on us despite our mess-ups and lapses in faith. When Adam and Eve sinned against him, he could have left them alone. He could have created a new man and woman, or even invented a new creation to call his workmanship. Instead, he chose to love us enough to make things right.

The world has always had an ebb and flow for God. Some have always followed God, and many have turned to and from him over the course of time. The Bible is full of living examples of God's people as they struggled to be the masterpiece God made them to be. Many prophets of the Old Testament were assigned to help the people of God correct problems of identity. Tribes and nations throughout history have altered what God created and formed it into something beneficial for themselves. We take what God has made and craft it into something for our own gain, our own recognition. But the Marys of the world continue to live the identity of masterpiece by doing what they can to give God the glory.

Sisters, we need to hear this serious warning. The labels that we accept as praise from other people can be *deadly* and heart-hardening. Sadly, many of the religious leaders who were around when Jesus taught completely missed who he was. Their hearts were hard, and why? The apostle John tells us that they loved hearing praise from other people more than praise from God (John 12:43). Their labels got to them, and their constant quest for approval cut them off from eternal life.

Our natural inclination to be recognized in this world can take our eyes off God, who has lavished us with gifts. For example, he has created beauty and put it inside each of us, but we have allowed it to become a competition. We have adjusted our gift of boldness and standing for what is right to be a defense for speaking our mind. These, and other labels, are distortions of our identity. They are places where we have been distracted from God's plan and purpose by the short-term benefits of this world.

Distraction alters our view of who we are created to be. God's gifts have been given for a reason. He created me and you to be unique masterpieces with living testimonies to his glory. Every distraction from our identity is a step away from living as God made us. And we need to remember that distraction can lead to death. When we stop and focus on our true identity, we can begin to live what Jesus calls a full life. When we see that we are made to have emotions, to be a leader who disciples many, or to be available to the people God puts in our life, we begin to reveal Christ to the world. We look less like the world and more like Jesus. Our reflection sets us apart as special. We become the woman God intended.

Identity in Christ is living. It's a life of rest and peace. It's a life of confidence and courage, instead of comparison. When we find our identity in Christ, we don't have to feel burdened to find it on our own. No glamour, no creating. Just living a life following God.

Redefining the Woman God Made You to Be

A woman of God is a person of confidence. She values herself because of her true identity in Jesus. She lives authentically. If we want to find meaning as women, we must relabel ourselves according to our identity in Christ.

We need to set aside the world and live as we were created. Live like Mary, letting people look at us sideways because of our choice to honor God above all else.

My journey to find what it means to be a woman of God has led me to redefine some of the typical labels the world casts on women. I no longer want to be beautiful or perfect because Instagram told me to be that way. I want to be beautiful so that the beauty of creation planted inside of me will show God's intricate design. I want to be popular so that others will hear me boast in the gospel. It is my hope and prayer that you, too, will join me on this walk to be who God created us to be. To be women who live authentic lives, not wanting to be the world's image, but rather the masterpiece of the creator God who loves us beyond comparison. If we want to be authentic women who follow Jesus, we must do what we can to glorify him. We must define ourselves by his definitions and act as reflections of God without regard to the approval of the world. We need to be brave women who define ourselves as helpers, created unique and with purpose.

Worldly labels are enclosing. They lock us into a place where we believe we should belong. We need to break down the barriers of being women who are "supposed to be," and start to build each other up as the unique masterpieces God created us to be.

Sisters, let us live according to who God made us to be and not who the world thinks we should be. Let us live a life of authenticity. Let us claim our salvation in Jesus with every move we make, not concerning ourselves with the world's judgment. God made us as unique, capable, and beautiful women. Let us redefine woman by God's definitions rather than the world's. And let us always be labeled "his."

Living a Labeled Life

How does it look to live a life labeled by his definitions? It's a life of authenticity. A life of reflecting God's goodness by living in a way that glorifies him more than it glorifies people. Living a labeled life is declaring to the world who we belong to without regard to who the world thinks we should be. Here is how you can practice living a labeled life:

- **Glorify God.** Let everything you do honor the God who created you. Consider everything a gift, and use it to let others know who God is to you.
- **Live authentically.** Don't compare yourself to others. Be who God made you to be instead of trying to be who someone else is made to be. Let others see you for who you are instead of trying to be who they want you to be.
- **Declare your salvation.** Let everything you do be a reflection of the one who died for you. It is only by God's grace we can be who he made us to be.

Discussion Questions

1. Discuss a time in your life when your perspective was changed. When did you realize you had to make a change in your thinking? Did you turn toward God's Word or away from it?
2. Do you look like one of your parents? Do you have children who look like you? How does your image of your parents or the image of your kids influence your behavior or attitude?
3. How do you see the image of God reflected in you? What will you do differently to reflect him now that you have participated in this study?
4. Name your favorite masterpiece and its creator. Why is it your favorite? If you are a masterpiece in God's mind, how does this piece change the way you see yourself?
5. Discuss a time you acted like Mary and did something to honor God that made the people around you look at you sideways. How did it make you feel? Imagine Jesus reacting to you as he did to Mary. Does that change the way you feel about the situation?
6. How can you live your life authentically, honoring God in everything you do? What are the distractions you face in living out your identity in Christ?
7. Look back at the prayer you recorded at the beginning of this book. In what ways has God changed your view of these labels?
8. How will you live a labeled life for God? What labels will you cast off, and what labels will you claim?